Echoes of War

BY
CHARLES MCCOY

AuthorHouse™
1663 Liberty Drive, Suite 200
Bloomington, IN 47403
www.authorhouse.com
Phone: 1-800-839-8640

© 2009 Charles McCoy. All rights reserved.

No part of this book may be reproduced, stored in a retrieval system, or transmitted by any means without the written permission of the author.

First published by AuthorHouse 5/28/2009

ISBN: 978-1-4389-4838-6 (sc)
ISBN: 978-1-4389-4839-3 (hc)

Printed in the United States of America
Bloomington, Indiana

This book is printed on acid-free paper.

Inquiries regarding purchasing copies should be addressed to Charles McCoy at the address below:

Charles McCoy
1809 Linda Lane
Jacksonville, AR 72076
Tel: 501-982-1495
E: chasrm@centurytel.net

About the Aircraft on the Cover:

This C-130 was the 126th Hercules built by Lockheed Aircraft Corp at Marietta, GA. It was accepted into Air Force inventory on 23 August 1957. It was assigned to the 314th Troop Carrier Wing, Sewart AFB, TN. Between 1964 and 1972, it served with the 51st Fighter Interceptor Wing and the 374th Troop Carrier Wing at Naha AB, Japan; and the 914 Tactical Airlift Group (AFRES) at Niagara Falls International Airport, NY. On 2nd November 1972, the aircraft was given to the South Vietnamese Air Force under the Military Assistance Program. On 29th April 1975, one day before the fall of Saigon, a South Vietnamese Major piloted the aircraft from Tan Son Nuit AB, RVN, to Utapao Royal Thai AFB. On board were 452 people seeking freedom. (There were 32 people on the flight deck alone.) Upon landing the USAF reclaimed their aircraft and in 1976 assigned it to the Oklahoma Air National Guard. The aircraft joined the 118th Tactical Airlift Group (ANG), Nashville, TN in 1979. It remained there until it's final flight to Little Rock AFB on 28th June 1989.

Foreword

My squadron that I was assigned to was in the process of phasing out the C-119 cargo aircraft, while receiving the new C-130s. There was no way to describe this new concept of a flying machine, it having jet engines attached to propellers, and could do the requirements faster higher and cheaper, except to do so we had to go back to school. Ashiya AFB located on the southern island of Japan called Kyushu, which occupies about 16,000 square miles. The end of the base runway on the north side faced the water, and mountains to the south. The scenery, even on cloudy days, would have been better than any painter could have hoped to capture on canvas.

Everyone used charcoal to cook with, and in the evenings the smoke from all the hibachi cookers just blended into the atmosphere to bring out even more high lights. By living off base, it did not take long to become part of the community and the people were as curious of us as we were of them. Our two young daughters with their blond hair always drew their attention, and at first it was nerve racking, when strangers wanted to feel of their hair. Only after we realized they had never seen blond hair before, did we know they meant no harm, and it actually bonded our people together to bring smiles and trust. My wife, kids and I lived only about three blocks from main-street of the town of Ashiya, and turning left two more blocks we were at the main gate of the Air Base. The average wage of the working people was only about $30.00 a month and we hired a maid for only $20.00. She only wanted $16.00 at first, but we offered more.

Preface

A non fiction story line of how it was lived with emotions of becoming a crew member, as a C-130 Flight Engineer. To bring together family life and Air Force life, with some joy and some sorrow as it unfolded. Written with hopes of going into high schools to inspire the young and give them the urge to want to be able to fly the planes and travel the world. This goes into some depth on maintenance fixes and problems in particularly C-130 aircraft. This could be good reading material for aircrew personnel. It also gives some understanding as to what politics has to do with service life, like getting fired by the First Lady of the United States. Except for not including "Elvis" (Which occurred before the start of the story) this book could just about be the "Forrest Gump" of the Air Force. To write about some of the events that happened, I had to go back in time in his mind to relive some bad times. Aircraft crashes and the trauma of the ongoing war or wars, I had to put myself back there and through some of the nightmares that would follow these experiences that had to be relived again and again, as if they were just echoes. Only these echoes brought with them the smells and screams as if they just happened again, only with fresh tears. This story I suppose actually started back about 1948. I was so fascinated with aircraft when I was 14 years old; I would ride my bike nearly two miles over the top of a hill, that over looked the Birmingham, Alabama airport. To park the bike, and sit on the ground for maybe an hour or so, just to watch the planes land and take off. At that time most of the planes were the war-birds that had survived the war. The passenger planes had been converted from military cargo planes. There

Charles McCoy

were some new planes coming on the scene too. I had just turned seventeen when I went with my friend Raymond to the Air Force recruiters for him to sign up. Sitting in the car got too cold so I went in to get warm, and I signed up too, for four years. Four days later, I was strapped in a converted C-47, and leaving the runway that I dreamed of, some three years before, as a passenger. After basic training, of all things, they assigned me to the aircraft maintenance field. The first school lasted six months, but it was just basic maintenance, but there was more to come. For each aircraft you worked on, you had to go to further schooling for that particular type. So it went, from C-54s, to C-119s, then to C-130s. This latest bird was the Queen of the crop. It also put me stationed at Ashiya AFB, Japan where we were getting brand new planes. This story takes up here, where my whole squadron was going to be in training, not just me.

CHAPTER ONE

Indoctrinated as a C-130 Flight Engineer

The year was 1959, and we just received the C 130 aircraft, and we felt like we had just got a new Cadillac, when compared to the C119s, that we were transferring out. I felt like I was lucky to be picked from maintenance mechanics, to go into flight engineer training. There were several of my buddies, including myself that we thought we were special because our aircraft we had been acting as crew chief on were the best in the squadron, and we were picked because of that.

Most of the engineer trainees, while going to class everyday, had their families over here, in Japan (the married ones including me) and most of us lived in the same areas off base. It seemed that we were all in the same boat, and since the only TV shows spoke only Japanese, we were drawn together more like families, and in the evenings there would be two or more families visiting, maybe just playing cards, having dinner, or maybe coffee, or beer. It was also a good time for the guys to go over what the class had covered that day. We also had a questionnaire book, which had to be filled out by each of us, by the time we finished our formal class training, simulator, and

Charles McCoy

flight training. It consisted of every system on the new plane, and covered everything you could possibly think of doing in case something went wrong, and the remedy of fixing it, or making a decision, to go or no go, keeping safety first above anything else. These people were to become life- time friends, to realize later in life, but that's getting ahead of the story.

This one couple in particular, Walter and Beverly Tramel were real close friends of my wife Wanda and I. Walter and I had been working and going to training together, from the day we both arrived at this base. Both of us had taxi and run up-license, and one afternoon, Walter came over to my plane, and wanted to know if I would ride the co-pilot's seat with him on a high speed taxi check, down the runway, and keep his wings level? We got clearance from the tower, and started down the runway. Walter laughed and told me over the intercom, "Watch this." as he pulled back on the steering column. We were doing about seventy-five knots, and were fast enough to raise the nose gear off the ground. At that moment the tower came in loud and clear, "That s a little high for a taxi check –Sergeant". Walter reduced the throttle, and the nose wheel made its landing noise as it touched pavement again. I still remember his giggle over the intercom, and the relief I felt at that same time that I thought for a second, we were not air-born.

There was not one failure in our class of trainees. So we were all set to go to the altitude chamber, but while we were in the large canister on the way up to a setting of forty thousand feet, we had oxygen masks on, I was thinking, "This is not so bad." Then we started down, and it felt like my head was coming off, and a swarm of ants were attacking my legs. I grabbed my legs and went through the motions of knocking the invisible creatures away. They leveled the dropping of the altitude, and I had an operator that was inside the chamber at my side, to see if I was ok. I had no idea of what was going on with my body. They adjusted the rate of descent to a much slower rate, which still was very uncomfortable. When they opened the door and let us out, a Flight Surgeon was checking me out before I knew what was happening. It was determined I had a head cold, and would not be able to go back up, for the rapid decompression demonstration we were required to have, in order to graduate. The Flight Surgeon saw that I was about to panic, because I thought I would be kicked out of the program, he came to my rescue when he came up with the word "Waver"! This same word, in the coming months, I found out to be a very powerful tool to be able to get around rules and regulations, and do things the way you wanted to do in the first place.

Our next step in becoming a flight engineer was to go through the flight simulator, while at the same time, we were getting some flying time of just riding along with instructor engineers. Some new pilots were enduring the same tasks we were, and all of us were getting to know and understand each other. A few of these pilots were cross training from C124 aircraft where the flight deck was about twenty- eight feet above the ground. It was quite an experience to have the aircraft that high above the runway and have the throttles pulled back, which made the aircraft, seemed to convert to a helicopter. That is what crossed my mind, instead of screaming. We would hit the runway very hard to which I came to believe this was a tough bird to be able to take a pounding like that.

One cloudy afternoon, I was on my way home from work; I pulled over to the side of the road and parked my car. A C130 was what we called making touch and go landings. It would come in to look like it was going to stop, but then the instructor pilot would call for a go around. The student pilot would then attempt to make the take off again. Normally, the student pilot was supposed to tell his instructor, "Flaps to fifty!" Then go to power for take

Charles McCoy

off, but this was not happening. At lease the flaps did not move from the 100% setting that they had used for landing, and with the power advanced for take off, the back of the aircraft raised first. The nose wheels were still on the runway, like they were glued to the pavement and the aircraft was up to take off speed. With this configuration it would have been hard to control the plane. At about three forth of the runway gone, undoubtedly the instructor pilot, (IP) must have pulled the flaps to fifty percent, and up popped the nose, and around they went for another touch and go. I sat in my car and observed about five more tries. Each time, same action, same setup, and I thought I'd sure not want to be setting in that engineer's seat. It looked like the wings were waving every-time they started their take off roll. I started my car and went on home to call it a day.

Next morning, I walked into our squadron's coffee shop located next to our maintenance office, and all the talk was about the accident the day before. The plane I had been watching shoot touch and go landings, seems the number four engine's prop had struck the runway about ten times, before the engine had literally broke in half. Parts had gone everywhere, including the other engine, and into the fuselage on the right side of the plane. Just by luck, the crew got the plane stopped, and no one got hurt. The student pilot was a cross trainee from another plane, where he had been an instructor pilot on that type, and for some reason could not remember to call for flaps to fifty. He got a reprimand, and the IP that was in charge of that flight, lost his IP rating, and was removed from flying. He had been the most liked IP in the squadron, and one that had more flying time, and probably knew more about the C130 then any man we had in our outfit.

As time seemed to fly by, we were in the process of getting our minimum required amount of flying time with an instructor engineer. Our schedule

Echoes of War

one day, included both Walter, and myself to leave Ashiya AFB, and fly to Okinawa, land, let one of us off, and the other student fly over water for an hour, land again, swap, and the other go for the next hour. Walter told me, "I tell you what, you fly in the seat down to Okie, get off I'll take the first hour, and you take the next hour, then I'll fly the seat back to Ashiya" It Sounded good to me. We landed at Kadena AFB, where they let me off, so I went into the flight line snack bar. They were using green back money, and all I had on me was three bucks. I bought a hamburger and coke, and the change that was left, I took in nickels. As I walked out of the door there were three-nickel slot machines. I put one nickel in, and hit the jackpot for thirty-seven bucks. A guy came over and was in the process of paying me, and I dropped another nickel in each of the other machines, to the tune of two more jackpots. As soon as I was paid, I had enough time to go over to the BX, where I got the wife and kids some surprise gifts. I was back to the flight line in enough time to meet my plane, and they could not believe I had hit three slot machines with fifteen cents.

Their flight had been low level, over water, and Walter looked kind of funny. He told me that the swells were so high, and the ride was up and down, so he put on an oxygen mask for the heat was miserable. They were even picking up surf through the coffeepot's overflow drain line, and it was blowing all over the cockpit. The aircraft commander told all of us, that the sea was too rough today, so let's go home. On the way back Walter told me he had really got sick, and would have to clean his mask. I could not help but laugh, and he said, "That's ok, your time will come!"

I got to ride the seat on the flight back home, and we were about 24,000 feet, and the air conditioner just seemed to stay on the warm side. I kept trying to nudge it cooler, when all of a sudden the small center glass over the pilots

Charles McCoy

left shoulder shattered with a loud pop. The quick emergency fix was to go to a higher cabin altitude, and lower the differential pressure so there would be less chance of the glass blowing completely out. When all was said and done, Walter asks me "Did I see somebody's hand shaking?" Guess I got paid back quicker than I expected.

Time was marching on, when one afternoon, after dinner, Walter and Beverly stopped at our house for us to catch up on trying to get the engineers question book filled out. Walter was all excited when he first came through the door and said, "Chuck I've found out how to make five thousand dollars! All you have to do is to be on the first C-130, that ditches in the ocean, and live to tell about it." It was just a rumor someone told him that Lockheed Aircraft Co. was suppose to have said. (This was the company that had made the C130s.) We all had a big laugh, and decided it would not be worth the effort, so we both got a cold beer and washed the thought from our minds.

The day finally came when the flight instructor told me and another student we were ready for our check ride. I still lacked about three pages in the Engineers Question Book. He told me I would have plenty of time on the flight, for it was an eight- hour cruise control flight. We would take off, go to altitude, reduce the throttles, and just more or less hang there for eight hours. That should be enough time to finish my book, and only one of us would be riding in the engineer's seat at the same time.

My seat time came up first, so for the take off, and first four hours it was my time to go through the questioning and answer game, to find out if I had retained any of the previous months of hard work. It seemed that all of my answers came out of my mouth automatically to my own surprise.

The other student came into the cockpit area, and I went down into the cargo section to finish my required questionnaire book. I sat down in a troop seat just forward of the right main gear wheel well area. I opened my book, and had one of the three pages completed, when while I was reading the next question, the page turned red, right in front of my eyes. At the same time I became aware of the awful smell of hydraulic fluid and my paper and I was being sprayed from a panel right behind me. One of the line fittings had burst open, and it was spewing fluid into the air, and going everywhere. I jumped up and ran up into the cockpit and very smelly and excited, told the flight crew. The pilot told me to go back down and find out exactly what line and what hydraulic system was the leak located. I was talking to them over the inter-phone system, and it was no problem to relay the news back to the flight crew.

In the meantime I'm hearing every thing being said in the plane. The pilot was coming out with some pretty choice words, telling the co pilot to get off a mayday, the engineer to go to emergency depressurization, and this damned plane won't go down. We were flying at twenty-six thousand feet. They had turned off the hydraulic system, and I saw the leak had stopped, so I was on my way back into the cockpit, when all of a sudden we seemed to have sucked in a cloud, not fog, but a complete cloud! Ears were popping, and it was hard to see, and I'm still headed for the cockpit. I'm not for sure where I got the portable oxygen bottle, or if someone handed it to me, but as I pulled in fresh air from the bottle, everything started to kind of come back into focus.

The scene in the cockpit was utter panic. We were still at altitude, the pilots were both pushing on the control column, the pilot was cussing, the co pilot was on emergency radio and screaming, "Mayday, Mayday," over and over! Then the pilot told the instructor engineer to turn the two safety wired switches that controlled the hydraulic systems off that was to his left behind the cockpit windows.

Charles McCoy

The engineer cut the wires, flipped the switches to off, with no hydraulic pressure to the flight control services, the auto pilot kicked itself off, that they had been trying to override. The aircraft went into a sharp decent, to feel like we were going straight down. Now we were really in trouble. With both the hydraulic systems turned off, there was no power to the control packages. We were strictly on manual control, and both pilots were doing their best to pull back the control column. The co pilot was screaming over the radio still, " Mayday…Mayday!"

We were passing through eight thousand feet, but still the control column would not respond to be manually obeyed. I could only think, "I can't swim!"

The pilot all of a sudden came out with the order to the flight engineer, to turn those hydraulic switches back on. As the switches were thrown, the life seemed to come back into the control column, and we could feel our body weight getting heavy, and since I was standing, the more leveling out we became the "G" forces drove me to the floor into a sitting position. It was a good feeling, and I did get a look at the altitude indicator, which was reading twenty-one hundred feet when we finally got leveled out. Believe me, that is a long way down from twenty-six thousand feet!

They had used the individual hydraulic pump switches located in front of the co-pilot, on his instrument panel, to shut down the system with the leak. We were flying on the other two pumps, and it was enough to satisfy the autopilot's need, which had been overlooked when we needed to start down. With the aircraft going into a rapid decompression, and everyone having to go on oxygen, the little old autopilot switch was simply overlooked. Someone said, "I'm glad we were not flying at twenty-three thousand eight hundred feet!" I finally figured out we would have ran out of air there too!

Echoes of War

Iwo Jima answered our mayday, which happened to be about fifteen minutes flying time, and gave us their heading, and ok to land. I think all of us gave thanks, when we turned and off in the distance could see the lights of the runway, and their rotating beacon flashing green then white.

Taxing behind a follow-me truck they led us up to be Base Operations building, where they parked us, and the ground personnel plugged in portable power units. As soon as we had electrical power, our engines were shut down. The loadmaster opened the front door, which let down and also contained built in steps. At the same time the door was in place a very large air policeman came running up the steps with an M-16 carbine held toward all of the crew that had made it down from the cockpit. This was the first time I had saw a police badge, or at least was aware they wore them. We were instructed to take our military ID card out, hold it in our hands, with our hands over our heads, and to come outside and form a line, and for GODS sake do not run or take our hands down, or we would be shot on the spot!

We went as instructed, and it was a very dark night, but as our night vision improved, we could see men standing about fifteen feet apart all the way around our plane and all had M-16s and pointed right at us. These guys meant business, even though we came in as an emergency, we came unexpected, with this base and their mission we found out later was classified.

After they figured out we were the good guys, and on the same side, they backed off. We were then able to shut the plane down for the night, and get a message off to home base, so they could send us some parts, in order to get back there the following day. Everyone then seemed to be extra nice, and even the Tech sergeant, who also was the fire chief, there was especially very talk-able. He also let it be known anytime we came back in to Iwo, he would

Charles McCoy

be glad to buy any extra whisky we might have on board. This place had its own bootlegger, but he seemed like a nice guy.

The next morning we awoke from a very sound sleep, to find a temperature and breeze that made me think of Hawaii weather. They escorted all of us, from the plane, to the chow hall, and the meal was great. The chow hall I found out to be one of the better places to relax, and enjoy your stay while at this island.

Leaving the chow hall, and not far in the distance, there was Mount Suribachi, the volcano where the flag raising took place, during world war two. In the morning sunlight, it was a sight that you could never forget, after remembering back to the day when our radios were telling about the battle taking place at Iwo Jima.

Our parts were supposed to be coming down on the aircraft that was to relieve another plane that had been on standby there for a week. When it did get there, they had also brought a ground mechanic to remove and install the new part. While this was taking place our instructor flight engineer was going through the final check off columns, and checking our book to qualifying both my fellow student, and myself as certified C130 Flight Engineers. After which we walked over to the other plane that had been relieved of standby duty, and parked besides our plane. We had plenty to talk about to S/Sgt. Foster, the engineer on that plane, about our in-flight emergency of last night, and nearly going into the ocean.

We got notice the plane was ready and our take off was to be thirty minutes before S/Sgt Foster's. We told him we would see him back at home base. This trip I was feeling pretty proud to be sitting in the seat, and not being asked about my job, but talking with the pilots about the situation of the previous night, and just what we should have done differently.

Echoes of War

After we had landed, and engines were shut down, I was helping the crew chief tie his plane down. The rest of the flight crew was waiting for the crew bus to pick them up.

With a loud voice, our aircraft Commander screamed out, "Look at that crazy SOB, he is going to hit that fire-truck!" He was referring to the plane that was landing. The number one engine was stopped, and the other three had been put in reverse, by mistake, and going to max power, throwing the aircraft off the runway. Their speed was excessive enough to see they were too fast to stop before hitting the fire truck that was in their path. The noise from the engines and props, wheels and tires roared, and the dirt was being thrown in front of the plane, and I'm sure the pilot was unable to see. We expected to hear an explosion, but instead the three remaining engines and props changed sounds, came out of reverse, went to max power, at the same time, the nose came up, and they were flying.

Just by a few feet, they cleared the fire truck, but they were just hanging by their props. They had to be only going about seventy-five knots, and below minimum control speed. (Speed when flight controls, steers the plane) Only about sixty or seventy feet in the air they missed the aircraft parked on the wash rack, where a mechanic was changing an anti collision light, on the very top of the rudder. He was seen taking a total of three steps on his way down.

The left wing started to drop; at the same time the doomed plane cleared the parked plane on the wash rack. By now they were over a part of base housing, in a left turn, and the three engines at full throttle. Left wing pointed straight down with the aircraft sinking. Just then they cleared base housing, but the housing was in like a small valley, and the ground rose up to meet the left wing tip, dragging it across the road. Sparks begin to shower from the

Charles McCoy

contact of metal and cement as the plane's left wing tore through the barracks just a few feet from the road. By a quirk of fate the fuselage cleared the top of the barracks and the cockpit went down between the second and third barracks. The right wing and number three and four engines dove straight into the top of the third barracks at full power. The cockpit was literally flipped up into the air, and the whole fuselage was traveling tail first, and crashing to the open ball field, after clearing the last barracks.

All three barracks were on fire, and people seemed to be running in all directions. The plane had its cockpit mostly ripped apart on its left side, but was sitting flat on the ground. From the back of the cockpit, the fuselage was laying on its right side and the right horizontal - stabilizer gone, and the left stabilizer pointed straight up. One part of the right wing was lying up and resting on the fuselage, and it was in the process of exploding and being ripped apart. One of our guys in our squadron was seen running into the gap between the cockpit and the fuselage, and after a brief period of time, he was out again holding the flight engineer under the armpits, but also was holding him over his own head, while at a full running speed, and saving his life.

Talking about it later, S/Sgt Ollie Olson, who pulled out the engineer said he had been on the field, and ran to the side when he saw the plane coming toward the barracks, just to see what was going on. After the plane came to a stop, he said people came running from inside the plane, but he could hear someone inside still screaming for help, and he said that he knew he had to take one look inside, so he went in. He found the engineer still strapped in his seat, and not being able to move very much. Reaching over the back of the seat, he was able to unbuckle the seat belt, and the only way he could get a good hold of the engineer was under his arms, so he grabbed him, and picked him straight up over his own head, turned around and ran. He said that at

Echoes of War

that time he had no time to even think about the weight he was caring, or how he was holding him.

There had been nine men on the plane, only the pilot, and nine men in the three barracks were killed. The flight engineer had some ribs broken, and some minor injuries, and even though he had been sedated at the base hospital, they had an air-policeman guarding his door to keep him in his room. He was at the top of his lungs, cussing and repeating over and over," Let me up, I've got to get that SOB, he reached between me and the co-pilot and grabbed the throttles away from the pilot and would not let go!"

He was talking about a passenger riding in the cockpit, who panicked when the pilot had reversed the three engines upon landing, sending the aircraft off the runway. He also was the same man that was the one student pilot who tore off the number four engine the day I had stopped to watch on the way home from work. He got a reprimand from that deal, now ten men lay dead.

To look at the crashed plane, it was hard to think that just a few hours before this had been the same aircraft that Sergeant Foster and I stood in front of at Iwo Jima. Also that he and anyone could have survived after plowing through three two- story barracks, which now were just ruble and still burning. I believe every one of the fifty-pound fire extinguishers that had been on the flight line, now sat around the burning buildings, empty of their contents. It occurred that all the fire-trucks and firemen were pouring all their attention on the burning aircraft, and not the buildings, even after it had been established that all people that had been on the bird had been accounted for. It was the next day, and after the fires were out, that the reason was the main part of the plane was lying partly on top of the large fuel lines

Charles McCoy

and valves that came from the base's fuel supply. If they had ruptured, then no telling what would have happened.

Our squadron tried to get everyone together on the flight-line at our squadron's coffee shop to have a roll-call that would last on into the night. Nine men that had lived in the barracks, never answered, and never will. Some of the men who had been in town and just sort of wondered in, could not understand why all of a sudden they were grabbed and were riding around on the other men's shoulders, which up to the time they walked in, they had been considered dead.

About 1900 hours (7 PM) the American Red Cross showed up and set up free hot coffee, and gave each one of the ones that smoked three packs of cigarettes (That had ten cigarettes in each pack) If anyone was hungry they were selling cinnamon rolls in C ration cans, for thirty-five cents. Keep in mind that everything these guys had was what they had on! Everything else had burned in the barracks. Around 1945 hours (7:45 PM) the Salvation Army arrived, and they had free hot meals, coffee, drinks, and issued each smoker two cartons of cigarettes, also gave each man that had lived in the barracks $18.00 cash toward buying soap, or tooth brushes and any small items they might need.

I had been scheduled to be on the first plane out to fly some of the injured to bigger hospitals. Sometime during all of this excitement, I had managed to run to my house to check on my family, because the crash had occurred about the time my wife would have been checking mail at our mail room that was in one of those barracks. They were fine, and I told my wife I was to fly out on the first plane. I remember her asking, "Why are you shaking so bad?" I was a ball of nerves, and could not control the shakes.

When they set up the coffee pots, there was no way I could hold a cup of coffee. I was not by myself either, for I knew all nine men that were killed.

20

Echoes of War

My buddy Walter came over and told me he had me taken off the schedule because I had just got back off a flight, and he was taking my place, and for me to go home.

The next day I still had the shakes, and the Flight Surgeon saw me at the squadron's break room, and put me on DNIF (Duty not including flying) He also gave me a bottle of pills to calm me down. I had never experienced anything like this.

It was nearly two weeks before I started to get back to a normal heartbeat, and the Doctor released me to fly again. I talked to my Instructor Flight Engineer and he set me up on a four hour flight for the next morning. I told him I had my doubts if I could do it, and he said, "If it will help, I will meet you out there and go up with you." I remember telling him "Thanks, and I would see you tomorrow!."

Sure enough, as I got to my aircraft, there he was and he went right behind me as I went through the before flight inspection. He kept assuring me that I had no problem. Right up to when we had all four engines running, and I felt his hand on my shoulder, and then he said, "I'll see you when you get back!" With that he turned and went down the steps.

I must have looked pretty weird, and the Aircraft Commander, sitting there told me over the interphone, "No sweat Sarge, I've got your back!"

Only about ten minutes in the air, I knew I was ok. Four hours later when we landed, my Instructor met us, and I told him "THANKS!"

I was just fine after that, and really enjoyed my job, and flying. My pilot, was an instructor pilot, and in my book a physic. He seem to know just what the student pilot was going to do next, and beside being a nice guy, he knew what this C-130 could do. It turned out that our job was to show all of the other pilots in our squadron just exactly how, and what happened inside the

Charles McCoy

cockpit of the plane that went through those three barracks. First we had to get above 15,000 feet, that being the minimum altitude we were allowed to shut down an engine. Then we shut down number one engine, and feathered the prop, so that it would not rotate. Then the student pilot could set up an imaginary runway, say 15,500 feet, and with landing gear down, and flaps to 50%, he would start reducing the power as though we were landing. With speed decreasing to around 80, or 85 knots, and our altitude about 15,550 feet, he was told, "Now, go around!"

First thing they all did was push the other three engines to max power, and just as quick, the left wing began to drop, and the aircraft would go into a left turn, and starting to drop. The IP would tell the student that he had the plane, and all he had to do was to bring number four throttle back, and the plane would nearly right itself.

We would set up again, and this time the IP would tell the student to pull power off number four engine, and he could recover the aircraft. That was the way it happened until we had all of the flight crews checked out.

Chapter Two

Following the Chain of Command,
God, the Pilot and Me

As days came and went Wanda and I was getting to learn the customs of life here in Japan. One afternoon I came home from an overnight flight, and noticed her grinning from ear to ear. She told me, "There will be no more driving problems off base for me." She said. "Today when going down the road, I met this man driving one of those three wheelers, and instead of me stopping, when it looked as he was going to run me off the road, I looked to my left. When I looked back, it was him in the little drainage ditch, and not me so I have it figured out."

She had no more fear of driving off base after that, and she did come up with some funny stories after that about how they drove over there.

One night after supper, Walter and Beverly were at our place for coffee, when Walter was telling us about flying into a thunderstorm. He said his ice warning caution light came on, and it was in automatic mode, so the system would turn the deicing system on. It was routine for the flight engineer to

Charles McCoy

tell the pilot that you were in ice, and the system was working ok. The pilot was an instructor pilot, and asked Walter what he had said. Walter said he repeated his information, but the IP's interphone must have been set too low, and the same question was asked, and answered two more times. Walter said the IP just turned and pulled his head set back, and loudly asks Walter again. Walter said he did not answer, but instead pointed to the yellow ice light. The IP reached up, and pulled the number two engine's emergency shut down "T" handle, and reduced number three engine's throttle. The IP then took up the conversation he was having with the student pilot, before like nothing happened. The ice warning light was located near the handle.

Walter said they must have flown about ten minutes, when the IP got his interphone to working, and ask him what did he think caused the fire light to come on?

When Walter told him there was no firelight, it was only the ice light. The IP got red faced and ask him why did he not stop him? Walter told him. "Well, I thought you knew what you were doing sir!" Then by the checklist they restarted the engine. The rest of the flight was enjoyable.

My crew, seem to end up on a schedule run for several weeks in a row. We would be leaving the runway on Tuesday morning, making stops at several bases, to load and unload supplies through out Japan, spend the night at Misawa AFB, Japan, then next day in to Korea, for a couple of stops, then retracing our route back to home station. It was really scenic at times.

One flight in particular, we had just left Tachikawa AFB, near Tokyo, when I told our navigator, that it seemed like every time we went by Mt Fuji, I did not have my movie camera, and when I did, like today, we did not even come close. Just then the navigator gave the pilot a new compass heading, and grinned at me and whispered, "Get out your camera!"

26

Echoes of War

We were approaching the top left side of Mt Fuji, and about two thousand feet higher than the mountain, when our pilot ask the navigator, if we were on the right heading? With a corrected heading, the pilot dipped the right wing, and we swung right around the top of the crater, as if it was planned. I made a great movie that day I will always treasure.

Another day, on the same type mission, we had just gotten about half way from Japan to the Korean coast, when our air-born radar system quit working, and we went to ground control for guidance. After about ten minutes, they called us, to be prepared to turn south and go to max air speed, that we had a Mig bogie about five miles off our right wing, going the same direction we were. A month before, there had been a navy plane shot up pretty bad. We flew the next twenty or so minutes, looking out our right side windows, wondering and hoping this guy was not the trigger happy red pilot from the month before. Then the all clear from ground control, "Your buddy turned north!"

Early one morning, I had drawn the ASAP, (As soon as possible) stand-by crew, and arrived at my plane to pull the preflight inspection. After the aircraft was inspected, it was set up for an alert status, for a quick start, and immediate take-off, in case there was an emergency somewhere in our area. No one was allowed in the roped off parking spot, where it set for the next twenty- four hours, if we did not get the call.

In the meantime, our crew had down time at home, but that is where we had to stay, and go nowhere. The alert call came through at eight o'clock that night. We were to go to Okinawa, pick up a doctor, and nurse, also an incubator, then to Formosa to pick up a new -born baby, take it to a hospital in Tokyo.

We had all four engines running, and taxied to the runway, using just the two taxi lights located on the main landing gear doors. We got clearance

Charles McCoy

to go on the runway to the north end, and the pilot decided to use the over run for take off, since we had maximum fuel in our tanks. Just as he started to make our turn around, he told me to kill the taxi lights; he was going to use the runway lights for take off. We were about half way in the turn, and I did as instructed and flipped the switch. We finished our turn, as we were lined up perfect in the center and nearly had eight hundred feet of over run, before we would even get to the runway. Parking brakes set, we sat there in the dark, awaiting clearance from the tower. Finally, they said go; our pilot pushed all four throttles to max power, the front of the plane dipped down about a foot in height from all the strain of those big engines. Then upon releasing the brakes, we were sucked back into our seats as the plane made its way up to speed. There was no dip between the over run and the runway, but there came some loud banging sounds, and I relayed to the pilot our props and engines were good, and we continued our take off. After double-checking all the instruments, I went to the cargo compartment, to see if the noise had come from there. Using the on board portable spotlight, we looked out the side windows at the engines, but they were normal, and no sign of damage. Back to the flight deck, I told the pilot, that every thing seemed good, and I had no idea of where the noise came from.

We made our stop in Okinawa, without shutting the engines off, picking up our doctor and nurse, also their equipment, and then on to a base in Formosa. After landing and getting to a parking spot, they did have a portable power unit that we could plug in for electric power, so we had lights without having to run our ground jet power unit, called the GTC. Then their fuel truck arrived, but it had no single point for hook up to our aircraft. I had to go up on top of the wing, and drag the hose up with a rope. Then as the wing I was putting the fuel into got heavy, and started to get lower, I had to lower

28

Echoes of War

the hose, then go to the other side, go through the same thing, dragging up the fuel hose, pumping until that wing got to low. I remember doing this at least two more times, until my tanks were full again.

Coming off the top of the wing, and back inside, the doctor told me that our iron lung electric plug in would not fit his incubator plug. I told him I could wire around it, but he said the baby was running out of time, that we needed to get started. When I ask him how warm did the baby have to be, he told me, at least ninety -eight degrees. I knew there was plenty of heat, in the cargo section, but I told him, if we had to, he could bring the baby into the flight deck.

After take off, and nearly to cruise altitude, the doctor came up on the flight —deck, with his shirt off, and his T-shirt wet, and when ask "How warm was the baby's temperature?" He replied," Ninety -seven degrees, and that was good.

The baby did well, and we dropped our passengers in Tokyo, and had enough fuel to make it back to Ashiya. It was a little after eight in the morning, and we were beat as we touched home base again. The ground crew met us, and our crew took off for a well -earned crew rest. I had just gotten home, and got sound asleep, when the phone rang, and it was the chief of maintenance, and he demanded I come up to the flight line now! He sounded mad, but I had to go see what he wanted.

He was sitting in a jeep, and told me to get in. On the way out to the plane I had flew on all night long, he wanted to know what in the world did we do to his aircraft, while using a few bad words, he just made up, because I had never heard them before. At the plane, he told me to look at the under side.

Just right of the nose gear, there was a tear about three inches wide and about six feet long. Where it stopped, and over about four feet, another tear,

29

Charles McCoy

like the front one reached another good six feet long. It kept the same pattern, all the length of the belly. At the most there were six rips, and they looked awful.

At about the time it took for this to soak in, I told the chief, that we did have a loud noise on take off from here, so we had to have hit something then. We then got clearance from the tower, to make a run down the runway to check it out, in our jeep. What we found and fiqured out was the crash barrier had sprung up behind us, before we made our turn around, and after we turned off the taxi lights, it was too dark to see. We hit it going the wrong way, for the rods were bent all out of shape. The outside of the plane was also the pressurized area, and all of the tie down rings, and plugs had to be in place in order to maintain pressure, which we did. I suppose this satisfied the chief, he even drove me back home. On the way, I told him, it must have been God's hand under the belly of that flight, and it was not meant for that baby to die. He agreed.

I took on a new outlook about flying that day. I could now see, beyond the crash that had been hovering somewhere in the backside of my memory, and see some good that came out of this experience.

It was finally the day that our time came to move into on base housing. We were to wait until the base's painters, had painted the inside, before they would let us move in. We made an agreement with civil engineer section that we would paint it ourselves, when they said it would be another month, before they could finish it. They would only give us the wall paint, and told us when we had that done; we could have the rest of the trim paint.

The next morning, I went to get the paint. They did not believe me, that we were done, or how just the wife and I had completed the job overnight, when they had a crew, that took a month. The Sergeant and his whole crew followed me back to the house. They had never seen a paint roller system before, that I had bought from the Base Exchange. I got my trim paint, and the wife and I moved in two days later.

Everything was going great, our own base quarters were nice, and made you feel like you were back in the states, and it was equipped with a real bathtub. The one off base was a homemade job, with real small tile work that was a pain to clean. With new paint on the inside of our on base house, it looked like a new house.

We had a lady from town that we hired as a maid and we were able to get her a pass for on base work. She became more like a member of our family. She would baby sit for us, and she seem to love our two little girls. I found out one day when I was playing with the girls, that our maid had even taught them some Japanese words, when the youngest called me crazy in Japanese. We all had a good laugh, and realized that both our girls could speak two languages.

We were using MPC, (military pay certificates), and our maid, Yakuno, when she did the laundry, would never go through the pants pockets. That is until she was hanging them to dry. The MPC change, nickels and dimes, etc were all paper, and she would then check the pockets, and put them on the windows to dry. It was funny to look out the windows, and have money stuck to the glass.

Our Base had open house, and some of the local merchants were able to set up shops in the big hanger, and they boasted some great bargains. We had aircraft on display, and there was hot dog, and hamburger stands, and everyone had a swell time.

My flight crew got picked to fly formation with a C 119, and a C 47. I suppose the C 130, and those two made quite a sight from the ground. The

Charles McCoy

C 47 was the point, the C 119 on its left wing, and our C 130 off its right wing. The C 47 must have been at full speed, the C 119 maybe cruse speed, but we were pulled back to flight idle on our throttles, when we came over the base. It was like we were just hanging in space. For some strange reason, two of out engines starved out of fuel, and we had to break away from the other planes. We went through shut down procedures, and then back to the air start checklist. No more problems and I knew what Walter was going to say when I saw him again. Something like "Yea, I know, you were just trying to make the other two aircraft look good!" I think I had him figured out, for it is just about word for word.

My crew happens to draw the ASAP stand by, one day that was really a pretty day. Along about eleven that morning, we got the go sign, and within the hour, we were climbing to our cruise altitude, on our way to Yokota AFB, just outside of Tokyo. There we picked up another Airforce Navigator, along with two other navigators from the Japanese self-defense Force. As soon as we topped off our fuel tanks, and got some in-flight lunches to go, we were back in the air on our way to the Philippines. The B 50s that were normally used to fly into typhoons had some kind of defect that all B 50s had been grounded, and was not allowed to fly. The C 130 was the next best choice to take their place. So our crew was the "Test the Typhoons Crew". There was a large storm brewing just south of the islands, and it was our job to go in and inspect this thing so the people there would know what to expect. We had a lot of confidence in this Herkybird, as some folks nicknamed the C 130s. As we got farther south, we left all the pretty sunshine behind us, as we started getting into overcast skies, and into darkness.

Our own navigator was getting a free ride, and the three we had picked up was giving our pilot the compass headings to fly by. Our navigator came

Echoes of War

up by my seat, and said he could not believe what these guys were doing. They were working our course, each three ways, at the same time. It was a pain, just to keep track two ways, but these guys had us pinpointed exactly, and it was a confidant feeling to know we were in good hands. At this time we started picking up what a full-blown typhoon looked like on our radarscope that was located just above the center engine - instrument panel. Outside it was as black as night. This storm made a perfect circle of a bright orange light on our scope, and the closer we got the bigger it got.

The visiting Air force navigator briefed all of us on what we could expect, and when. Our altitude was 26,000 feet now, and we were to try and get over the tops of the clouds, by going up to 30,000 feet, fly to the center and descend into the clearing, at 2500 foot increments at a time. Each time, we would leave the clearing and go into the circle of clouds, they would take some readings, then back into the center clear area, and drop 2500 feet more, and so on into the depths of this huge whirlwind. He also told us we could expect one large bump in the road when we made our first encounter from the inner circle, and after that they could ease us in and out fairly smooth.

This guy knew what he was talking about, and he had lots of experience from flying the proven B 50 weather ships. Now was the question, how was this C 130 going to take this kind of weather?

We saw the outer ring on our scope get closer and closer, and seem to just ease by, as we broke out of the cloudy dark night sky, into a clear moon light night, and into the circle. It must have been two or three miles across that looked like a beautiful night. Dropping down the 2500 feet, we must have been holding our breath, as we sailed into the wall of swirling unknown of what was to come. As predicted, there was a bump, but not really what we expected. I knew my crew had been over bigger clear air turbulence, called

33

Charles McCoy

"CAT" before. (Clear Air Turbulence) Our typhoon Airforce navigator reported to our crew, that this was a sweet plane and he thought the C 130 would end up taking the B 50's place as a typhoon, and hurricane chaser. He gave out the course heading, and we were back out in the clear again. Making our own circle, dropping to the lower altitude, we could look down and actually see the ocean, which was solid whitecaps, and glowed in the moon -light.

It was quite a ride, going in and out of the calm center, and then back into the black unknown, but at best, it was not as bad as we might have imagined, thank goodness. Finally we had recorded, and sent the information on to the weather center. Then we headed back to home base. Our guest navigators could only brag about our aircraft all the way back, and how its response to the typhoon had been.

It was good to get back home, and into a regular flying schedule. Another flight engineer, who was the same rank as me, A1C, (Three stripes, referred to sometimes as Buck Sergeants), well we seem to fly mostly the four and eight hour local flights. The better missions, like to Bangkok, or to some place real nice went to the higher ranked engineers. That was just fine with me, because it put me on a more or less eight- hour day job, and that way I could get more family time in.

One week though, I had flown three eight- hour cruise control missions, and I had to complain when they had me on schedule for the fourth. That was too much, and my boss agreed, and changed my flight. It was a search mission for a Delta Dart that had ditched just southwest of Okinawa. Upon arrival at our search area, we had air speed set at 100 knots, and our altitude at 100 feet above the water. We also had three volunteers that were ground crew, because they wanted to help find this pilot.

Echoes of War

Flying on a grid pattern, it was back and forth, and as time passed, we still had all available eyes scanning the water hoping to maybe see a yellow raft or some kind of signal, from the downed pilot. We were not the only plane out there, and it made you realize that this was a big ocean. Finally we had to turn and go home, but there was hardly anyone talking, except our navigator giving our course heading to our AC. There was still a chance, that one of the other aircraft might locate the downed pilot. All we could do now was to hope.

A seagull's wingspan might measure between three and four feet across, and flying at 100 feet would make it about 1/8" wide when you were looking down on it. The color of the sea would also be about the color of a flight suit, and altogether at 100 knots it is not good odds. The only things we can do is to pray, and try our best.

CHAPTER THREE

Testing the C-130 beyond its specs

Just about the time my wife and I discovered that we were going to have another little one in our family, we found out the base was going to close. Our squadron was to move to Okinawa. We still had a few months before the closing was to take place.

I thought it ironic that my wife was from Oklahoma, and our first two children was born there, making this move to Okinawa, would therefore give us another "OKIE", in our family.

We had really started to enjoy our assignment here in Japan. My wife, Wanda was taking a language course on base to learn Japanese, and she had picked up enough to be able to understand what the locals were saying sometime in their conversations. One day, she just happens to laugh, when two clerks were talking about the American woman. They were shocked that she understood them, and that they had been talking about her. It had been a compliment though, and they ask her, "You understand Japanese?" Then all three had a good laugh together.

Charles McCoy

The clerks in the stores expected the customer to try and get their prices down to a lower price, and they would put on a show, but they did bring them down. It was enjoyable to just buy about anything.

There was one restaurant that we really enjoyed dinning at, and to remember back of what we were getting, it seems like from a dream world. They would have a Kobe beefsteak, with potato salad, and a boiled egg chopped up in it. Also on the same plate, there were fried potatoes, and a slice of rice bread. For a beverage, a small bottle of champagne, to round out the meal, included. The total charge equal was two American dollars, for each person. For a well- rounded menu, it did not compute, but the meal was delicious, and we made a habit of dinning there as often as possible.

Whenever we went down-town, and our two small blond headed girls beside us, a lot of the people would just have to touch their hair. It was unnerving at first, until we realized that they had never been around anyone with blond hair. They were also shocked and delighted to hear a few Japanese words come from their lips, when our children greeted them back.

Sense we were living in on base housing, we will qualify for direct base housing when we get to Naha AFB, Okinawa. They also told us it would be a quanset-hut, but it would be clean and nice, even though it was classed as substandard compared to the regular base housing. We would also be getting it for a discount on our housing pay.

We had to drive our car over to the Navy Base, to be shipped to Okinawa, so for a few days, we were without transportation. It was not a big deal, because we could just about walk anywhere on base, except with two small ones, and one on the way, we could use the base bus to get around, if it got too much.

Finally, the day arrived and they came and packed up our furniture, and we had to move into the base guesthouse for a couple of days.

Echoes of War

Our transportation was one of our own squadron's C 130 aircraft, and it was a first time for my wife and children to fly on one, that I considered was one of my flying offices. She said that it was too loud. It was a short flight to Okinawa, and the kids were really good, and seem to enjoy the trip. I suppose they remembered the plane ride from the States to Japan, twenty-eight months ago, but they were pretty small at that time, so maybe not.

We settled right in, after we had landed, and it was a short seventeen miles from the base at Kadina AFB, over to Naha AFB, on an Airforce bus. It took us direct to the base housing office, where we were assigned to our on base house. We also had to sign for the furniture that was already in the house. It was a three- bedroom quanset, and we figured out that the small bedroom should hold our furniture, that was on its way down, sense they said we could not turn in the furniture that was already in the house. Why, we will never know.

Our new home was sitting on a slight slope, and it sat back from the road by about sixty feet. Our sidewalks were made something like a forklift pallet, but were made up in long lengths, and at the front steps, there was a joining walkway off to the right. It went to the side, then turned to go to the screened in porch, half way of the house. I was still not certain if I would be able to live in a house that rounded over from one side to the other.

A few days later, Walter and Beverly showed up, but their house was off base in a military housing unit.

After getting settled in, we were still going about our daily flights, also it seemed that we were getting one week a month on classified standby duty. It was lonesome at times, because most of the time we were doing just that. We could go anywhere on base that had an alert bell, and our vehicles were painted white, with a red siren on one front fender. If the alert bell sounded, we had the right of way anywhere on base, and we had to be in the air within

Charles McCoy

minutes. One thing that came out about the drill, was it made you gun shy of loud bells.

We did go through practice drills sometimes two or three times each week we were on duty. It just more or less depended on how we made it through each drill, and how fast we could be in place. There were also signals we could see, that meant it was not a drill, but the real thing.

One day, during an alert, the signal system had a shorted wire, and I cannot began to express the feeling that ran through my mind, because this could mean the third world war, and possible the end of the world.

As flight engineer, it was my job, with the help of the load- master, to get the four engines running, and stay in place until the rest of the crew showed up, and the pilot would take over his seat.

Walter was on the same shift of standby duty, and as soon as he had engines on speed, he told the load- master to get in and close the door. He then taxied the aircraft out of its spot, and down to where the pilots and crew would be coming out of the compound running. To their surprise, there sat their plane with the front door open and all engines at idle.

Even though the signals were indicating this was the real thing, we were not suppose to move the aircraft, and Walter had a darn good argument that he was authorized to taxi, and there were nothing written on the subject. It turned out instead of taking all of our taxi license away; they said the enlisted men with their license could still taxi as long as the aircraft commander was on board. With the cargo we were caring, this turned out to be a very comforting decision that we all could live with.

Walter was a good sport, and I believe he enjoyed any kidding that came out of this, and I personally had it in my mind, out of all the flight engineers in our squadron, he was the safest to ride with. Especially after that day we high sped down the runway at Ashiya AFB, Japan.

Echoes of War

My crew turned out to be a training crew, to check out new pilots, navigators, and sometimes give check rides to regular crewmembers.

One day we had a couple of student pilots on board, and had taxied to the other side of the runway, to pull our engine checks, and also get clearance for take off. While we were waiting, there was a Navy twin engine P2V (Patrol bomber) aircraft pulled in close to our right wing, and parked, to do the same as we were doing.

Just as the tower was giving us the instructions to line up on the runway, there was a bright flash of light that had happened from the other side of the runway, coming from the area of parked F 102s. At the time it got our attention, we could see a lot of smoke and fire, with a rocket coming right at us. We lucked out, it missed us but hit one of the props on the P2V. The prop bent, and the rocket went through a chain link fence, and then hit a rock sea wall, that put it on out to sea. It never exploded, but it did a job on two flight crews. Also the crew chief that was in the process of loading the rocket got rolled about seventy-five feet and scratched pretty good, and some minor burns, we were told later. He had not pulled a check for stray voltage, before installing the rocket, which set it off.

We finally had our clearance for take off, and got into the air, where we felt safe after that ordeal. Only this day was not over by a long shot. Our student pilots were getting some instrument training that they had to put on a face shield so they could not see out the windshield when told to look up, and also take the controls of the aircraft. It was to see if they could right the plane to a level and safe flying attitude. This could only be done above 15,000 feet, where the plane could be in any position of flight, and the power setting could be in any configuration. After a few times of recovering they all seem to do real good.

The problem came to us when we had just completed their qualifying for that phase, and we were flying stright and level, and relaxed. We had

Charles McCoy

a shadow streak across the cockpit, and at the same time a Navy Crusader aircraft buzzed us going in the same direction as we were. We had his sound to add to our own few choices of words. This guy had a buddy that did his part of the prank too. As we looked for the first plane, his friend seems to go between the nose of our plane and the left wingtip, while going stright down, but also at a twisting motion. Both missing us, but scaring the heck out of each of us that saw him and when we got back to earth, our IP was going to write an operational hazard report on the Navy pilots, but one of his buddies told him not to do it. He said he had pulled a prank on the Aircraft Carrier the Navy pilots was flying from, and he and his C130 crew had set up a landing pattern on the Carrier the day before, and at the last minute broke away from their approach. So they were just getting even. We all had a good laugh on that.

The next day while I was in the process of making a preflight inspection on the plane we were going to fly, the Navy was still not through. My plane was on the parking ramp, which was east of the runway, when out of the blue came a Navy Crusader about fifty feet above the run-way, and a good three hundred miles an hour. At just the right moment, he released three photo flash bombs, that did not hurt anything, but the flash and noise was enough to scare the daylights out of everyone on the flight line.

I guess that was payback for the rocket shot, from the day before. I kind of thought maybe now the score was even.

Okinawa was a little different from Japan. We could drive on the right side of the road, but the speed was a max of thirty-five miles an hour. Our greatest fear here was the snakes, that they called "Habu", that were poisonous as a Rattler, but ten times meaner. If it bit you, it would do it four or five times. I tried to keep our grass cut real short, because I thought that would help keep them away. Wrong! Another man in my squadron had the same idea, but he had to call the Air Police to come shoot a five-foot Habu that was sun bathing on his lawn.

That's when I got the idea we needed a dog. I bought one from a local that bragged the dog's father was a French- poodle, and the mother was an Okinawa dog. I just could not turn down the sales talk. The kids were delighted, and he did do a good job, we never saw any snakes around our house.

Some of our flights took me back to Ashiya AFB, to pick up inventory material, and just about everything that could be moved from our old base to our new one. It was funny at times to see what the Japanese were doing to some of the items they thought were unnecessary. Things like they had filled the base's swimming pools with sand, the reason was there was the ocean right next to the base, so they did not have need for the pools. It was also weird to see smoke stacks coming from windows of base housing that had been heated from the base's central heating system. I guess charcoal and hibachi pots proved to be cheaper in the long run. Some days, we made two and three trips, back and forth, moving the equipment, from base to base. This turned into weeks before we finally got settled in to our new base.

One bright sunny Sunday morning, I had got stuck with a make up flight for this one student pilot, so he could get his landings under control. It was just the instructor pilot, the student pilot and I., no loadmaster, or scanner, and we were considered a minimum crew.

As we were taxing to the runway, the Major (IP) was telling us that his wife and children were having a picnic on a sandbar, just west of Kadina AFB, and before we started the flight lesson, he wanted to make a flyby first and sounded innocent enough to me. Wrong!

Charles McCoy

Take off was normal, and as soon as we were up to about one thousand feet, engine power pulled back to about one hundred knots, landing gear, and flaps up, we turned toward the sandbar. We could see his family waving, as we seem to glide into line with them in view. The closer we came, the lower we got to the water, until we were about one hundred feet high. Just as we were directly above them, the IP pushed the throttles to max power and set the flaps to fifty percent while pulling back on the flight controls. Leveling out at about two thousand feet, and flaps coming back up, powering back, he started into a tight circle. Completing a three hundred sixty-degree turn, he put the power back to max, dropped the nose down to point at that sandbar again. We began to double our airspeed, from one to two hundred knots, then three hundred, then fifty more. At two hundred feet altitude, we buzzed the beach, and he pulled back on the elevator control, which felt like we were in a rocket.

There was scattered puffy white clouds hovering at about five thousand feet, and we were headed for them, at nearly four hundred knots, and at a forty-five degree angle. Also we were crossing the landing approach for Kadina AFB runway. We entered the cloud, and were out the top in a matter of seconds. Our timing was perfect to barely miss the F 100 fighter, which was on his final approach.

From all the noise we had been making, it suddenly got quite in that cockpit, for we all had just witnessed a near death experience.

Finally the Major said, "Well let's get to work." He then turned the aircraft over to the student pilot, and said to head back to Naha AFB.

We were going to let the student make landings, which sounded all right. Wrong again! I thought the guy was doing pretty well, even though we seem to float down the runway another five or six hundred feet too much. I

Echoes of War

figured he was trying to make a smooth landing. After instructing about six landings, the IP was starting to come out with some powerful cuss words. He told the student that he did not have control of the aircraft, and that when he wanted the wheels to touch the one thousand foot marker, by God, that's what he wanted.

After two more tries, the Major took control, and in the process of going around again, he told us he would line up for landing, at one thousand feet altitude, come over the end of the runway, at that altitude, and touch main gear at the one thousand foot mark.

I don't know where my mind was at that time, but it sure did not register to what he had said, until much later. I was smoking a cigarette, and thinking about what a pretty day it was for flying.

We made our flight pattern, and getting lined to the runway, when the Major told the student pilot, that when I call " Flaps, you set them to one hundred per cent, and that's all I want from you, I will do the rest."

At one thousand feet, and our airspeed of just eighty knots, we crossed the end of the runway, and like clockwork, the Major said, "Flaps". At the same time, he pulled back the throttles, and pushed the control column forward. The aircraft obeyed, and we were in a dive, and it felt like the only thing keeping me from falling through the center windshield, was my seat belt and shoulder straps. I was looking stright down at the concrete runway.

Then the Major pulled back on the column, making the big bird pick its nose back up into a flying position. The main gear made a small sound as it touched the one thousand-foot marker, as the Major predicted.

The base tower called us and said, "No more down the mountain landings today." I thought to myself, "I would like to buy that control tower operator a steak dinner!"

Charles McCoy

We were on the ground, and taxing back to the end of the runway, when the Major asked me, " Sergeant, what are you doing?"

It was then that I realized that I had just lit a cigarette and my hands were shaking, but I did take another long draw off that smoke, before I put it out. The Major never got an answer from me.

CHAPTER FOUR

Clouds, mountains, instruments flying

Another nice day, here on the keystone of the Pacific that this island was sometimes referred as, and I had a day off. I got out our grill, and hot dogs, and I noticed our two girls had made friends with some neighbor's children. There was also a new friend, a large yellow Boxer named Judy. She belonged to a family who lived in the Navy housing, across the open field that was across the road from our house. I made friends with Judy, and all it took was a hot dog. Later that same day, but after we had gone to bed, and all of us sound asleep, we were awaken by Judy and our dog barking right at our bedroom window.

Remember that our roof was round, and that each window had an awning like frame, and the window hinged, so that it rose up and swung out. There was the screen, built that the window would clear, when opened. It was this screen that I had put my nose to, as I tried to see what the entire racket was about. At that moment, Judy saw her new friend, and she probably remembered I was the one who gave her the hot dog. She gave me a big lick,

Charles McCoy

on the other side of that screen, and it was so fast, and me half asleep, my feet left the floor, I flipped backward, clearing the full size bed and crashed into the oscillating fan. I don't remember what I said at that time, but it had Judy's name in it.

That hot dog made a big impression on that dog, for every time I stepped out the door, here come Judy. The first time, she started out as a small yellow dot and she was running from across that open field. The dot kept getting bigger, and bigger, and I had a class A uniform on, and when I recognized it was Judy, she was already in the air. My arms went out for some reason, and then I had about forty pounds of muddy Boxer, in my arms, and she just turned and I received another lick. That dog sure did like me! I remember having to check every time I went out side. Sometimes I could barely make it, while running to get in my car.

We did a lot of sight seeing on my days off, and there was a lot of history left over from the battle of Okinawa. Not far from our house, there was a large hill with a very large anti aircraft gun poking out from a cave like hole. This also happened to be the first target that our forces hit. It was like a tourist attraction. They had it put back together, and you could go inside the gun area and look around. The hole was like a large room, maybe forty foot across, and thirty feet deep. There was about three or four doorways that had been sealed up with cement and brick. It was down these cave wall corridors that led to ammunition storage rooms deeper in the hill.

Another tourist attraction, but grim was suicide cliff. The story was when the island invasion started, and they had decided they had lost; the young girls had all met at that spot. They were so afraid that when they were caught, the invaders would attack them; they more or less jumped off that spot, (Cliff) and into the ocean to their deaths.

Echoes of War

It seemed like every time I pulled my week of stand by over at Kadina AFB, just seventeen miles away, my wife could bring the kids over for dinner at the NCO club, or base cafeteria. Just like clockwork every time we would have the dinners put in front of us, the alert bell would sound off, and I had to leave the building running to go to my plane. Thank God, all we did was get engines going, and they would give us shutdown orders. Then we could put the engine quick start set up back in place. Sometime we could even get back to our dinner plates, and they would still be warm. I thought to myself, "Man, we are fast!"

There was one week of standby I remember well. I only had two more days and my seven days would be over, and I could go home. Wrong! Here came a typhoon, and headed straight for the island. We had to fly all the planes out and over to Korea. The typhoon slowed its speed, and took its own sweet time about getting past Okinawa. It was in and around the island for five days.

Meanwhile, my wife and kids are holed up in our Quonset hut and the shutters shut tight, only after the Fire Marshal had come by. He had chewed her out for the shutters not being closed. She explained to the officer, that being seven months expecting a baby, there was no way she could get out in that high winds to close the shutters. There was supposed to be someone from our squadron to have been by to close them. There was a man who came right out after the Fire Marshal got hold of our first sergeant, and he had also apologized to my wife.

Finally the storm had passed, and we could return to Kadina AFB. All our C-130s back on the ground, except for the last one, and it was only ten minutes out. Then all hell seems to hit at the same time. That last bird was on minimum fuel, and was going to have to land very soon, and on that island. The problem was there was an F-100 on the ground at Kadina, with an armed

49

Charles McCoy

heat-seeking missile under its belly, and the aircraft and missile was on fire. The control tower told the flight crew to fly over to the other island, just on the west side of Okinawa, and get behind that island, to fly as low as possible, and try to stay out of sight.

What saved the day was the tail end of that missile burned off first, and it did not get released from its position. Also they got the fire out. Then our last C-130 was able to land. My wife had some catching up to do on talking when I did get home. It was quite an ordeal to have been cooped up in a Quonset hut, with two small girls and expecting a baby, with a typhoon howling with rain and wind in excess of 85 miles an hour for nearly a week. What made it even worse was our address of 431C, was just two spaces away from where 431A had been wiped out earlier from a previous typhoon.

There had been a lot of damage, but I can't remember any casualties on the island this time.

After I had been home for a couple of days, my name came up for my crew to go to the Philippine Islands, to fly supplies to Formosa. We were spending the nights at the Navy base at Manila, and back and forth to a base in Formosa. Everything was going great, until that last day when right after take off our navigator reported to our pilot that our radar just went out. He gave all the right directions, and we ended up over our field at about twenty five thousand feet. We were in dense clouds, and everything outside the plane was dark gray. Our pilot said he was going to make an ADF approach, and set up to do just that. When we arrived at our marker, the needle on the ADF indicator swung around to point back to the station. The pilot pulled the throttles back, and we started our jet penetration, as he followed the ADF needle down into blacker and blacker clouds. All of a sudden there was a large sharp blackness right in front and just below us. I screamed into my microphone, while hitting the pilot's right shoulder, "Mountain!" He pulled back the control column, and we cleared the mountain by less than one hundred feet, and we also had gone to max power in the process. Our pilot had messed up royally on his ADF approach. He was suppose to have flown so many minutes after the needle swung, make a one hundred eighty degree circle, and come back for a second swing. This was to make sure we had the right signal, and not a thunderstorm, which we had followed a large storm at the most twenty five miles off course, and into the mountain range of eleven thousand feet high. We had reached nearly ten thousand, when the weather allowed us a peek, just barely enough time to save ourselves. After we got back some altitude, and we all had settled back down, our pilot apologized to all our crew, and explained as to how he messed up. He even said that if any one of us wanted to write him up for an operation hazard report to go ahead, but he assured us he would never make the same mistake again. That was good enough for us, and no report ever went in, as far as I know.

After that near miss, I made it a habit to pick up our landing charts sometimes in the flight, and look over what kind of terrain we were going to land at. To jump ahead of my story, I caught two different pilots turning the wrong way at the ten thousand-foot markers later on in flights that followed.

It was a very warm summer, and just right for typhoon season. We had another storm headed right for the island, and somehow it picked up speed and really had gotten to close when they told us to fly the planes out, and tie everything else down.

I had arrived at my assigned aircraft, and was doing a walk around inspection with the winds nearly blowing me down. It was blowing from the west, and our planes were parked facing north. I raised the right landing

Charles McCoy

gear door and set the mechanical rod in place to hold the large door in place, while I ducked into the wheel-well area to check required items prior to flight. Just as I bent over and under the door, there was a huge blast of wind that lifted the door all the way up against the side of the fuselage. The rod lifted off its resting-place, then the wind stopped, letting the door free fall right down across my back. Knocking the breath out of me, and putting me on the ground. I remember the pain and also that I had to keep holding my shoulders and head up and away from those two main tires that were snow type, and had wires sticking out of the threads. The wheels were moving back and forth from the pressure of the wind on the rudder, and I had the full weight of the landing gear door on my back. I had to crawl backward out from under that thing and I was laying in about an inch of rainwater.When I did get myself free and backed away about two feet my face was in the water. I was able to get my arm up and under my head to keep my mouth above water, I think I passed out for a time, and when I did come to my senses, I thought if I can stand up, my back would not be broke. I pushed my body up, and was sitting in the water. I really was not aware of the wetness, for the amount of pain I had, blocked out the dampness I was sitting in.

Finally I did get to my feet, then the thoughts started going through my head that this aircraft had to be in the air and away from this storm. We had sixteen planes, and only fifteen flight engineers. I did not know then that our squadron had signed a waver to allow a flight chief to ride with an instructor pilot and act as engineer on the extra aircraft. I got the crew chief to walk the rest of my inspection, and I made my way to the cockpit.

Somehow we got the engines running and taxied out toward the south end of the runway. The plane with the wavered engineer was right in front of us, and it had been going through a phase dock inspection. It had parts

Echoes of War

removed in the wheel well area, so the main gear was chained down and they had to fly all the way to Yakoda AFB, Japan, with their landing gear in the down position. This meant a much slower airspeed.

As the aircraft got clearance, to take the runway, our winds were coming at us at a steady forty miles an hour straight at the large rudder on the back topside of the plane. This action tried to even make the nose tire skid toward the direction of the in coming winds. The tower was trying to get the planes off the ground as fast as possible, and we were taking the runway two at a time. As the lead plane started his roll, the rear plane moved up one spot, to allow the next in line to fill his spot. This seemed to help control and make a difference in the speed of the crosswinds on driving the plane to take off speed. However, the plane with their gear chained down was just in front of us, and the pressure from the winds was so strong, we saw both right main tires blow out, at the same time their nose came up into the air, and they were flying. We were just about to take off speed ourselves and there was no stopping, for we knew there was another plane moving, directly behind us.

As soon as our wheels were in the air, everything outside the cockpit windows turned a dark gray, and the ride was bumpy, while the rain was unimaginable. We were in a climb, and I wondered to myself just how much pain a body could take. I had a flight suit on, and I unzipped it to my waist, and raised my T-shirt. The navigator took a look, and told me how red my back was, and there was some small cuts, but said he did not see any bones sticking out.

We continued our flight on into Yakoda AFB, and within an hour later the plane with the right tires flat made its landing on a foamed runway. The pilot did a nice job of holding the right wing up in the air until it was about sixty-five or seventy knots airspeed, and it suffered no major damage.

53

Charles McCoy

I knew I should go to the hospital, but all I could think of was lying down, and being still. Somehow, I got into my room after checking into the transit barracks, and I lay down after I had got out of my jump boots. I awoke next morning, still in my flight suit, and missing both supper and breakfast. The warm shower seems to take some of the pain away. Why I did not go get checked out by a doctor then, I'd never know. I was young and must have thought I was superman, and I was able to stand and walk around, so my back must not have been broke.

The loadmaster on my crew, and the crew chief, and myself went over to the base cafeteria and I made up for my hunger. We had four days at that base, and I stayed in my bunk nearly the whole time hurting with every movement.

Finally, word came that the storm had passed Okinawa, and we could return home. This had really been a trying time for me, and I kept thinking that the aches and the pain would get better. I think I was living on aspirins for the next few days, and my wife kept after me to see the doctor. I was able to go on to work, but I had to modify my duties to co exist with the pain that was walking around with me. Once I had made my walk around inspections before we took off, the rest of the time I would be sitting in the flight engineer's seat, so I thought. It was then that it became apparent to me that I could not sit for more then thirty minutes, nor could I stand up for even thirty minutes. At night I had problems getting to sleep, and then for about thirty minutes the pain would wake me back up. It was the simple things that were really getting to me, for I could not pick anything up like even a bag of groceries.

At long last I went on sick call, and after a few x-rays, the doctor told me I had bones broken, and one of the vertebras had a piece broken and separated and about a half inch away. It looked as if I had an extra short rib. He also told me to do some special exercises, to put a board under my mattress, to take the medication he prescribed, and to not lift anymore than five pounds for a year. I was also grounded and duties not to include flying.

My boss, the ranking flight engineer got pretty mad when I carried in my paperwork, because we were only authorized a certain number of engineers in our squadron, and we were short one man now. I stayed in quarters as too sore to walk around for about a week, and I suppose the physical therapy and medication started to kick in.

I had to report back to my duty station after the second week, and my boss thought up a plan of making me useful. I was to check the flight schedule every evening, and there was to be a backup aircraft every morning. I would inspect the backup plane that would take the place of any plane that could not make its takeoff time, or broke down at the last minute. The backup aircraft would have a rope around its parking area, and no one was allowed in the area, and the aircraft would be cocked for quick starts. He did not want even late takeoffs. It looked like my flying days was over for a while.

One good thing did crop up out of this ordeal, and after I had a pattern set for my new work schedule, it was nice to fall back into a family living again. There was no day off, but after I had my one aircraft inspected, I had to attend the pilots and engineers briefings, and then I was off. That led to too much off time, so my boss thought up these other small jobs to keep me busy. I did a lot of sign paintings of our squadron's emblem of a white unicorn with wings out stretched, with a blue background. These went in one of the little windows on the C130, right next to the pilot's left leg, on sixteen planes.

Next job he had me doing was to build some boxes that would fit in a pickup truck's front seat that the flight line's job controllers could use to keep

Charles McCoy

track of what was going on with the maintenance on the planes. These turned out pretty neat. The shape was like a breadbox, angled toward the driver, and painted black. It had clear plastic on its hinged lid, with lines grooved into the underside. There were also lights built into the plastic, so you could use colored grease pencils to write on. At night it made your colored letters stand out like neon lights, and also had a dimmer switch. Inside they could keep extra forms and whatever. It caught on so well that I ended up building one for each squadron's flight line truck. It was really a light duty job.

One of the men in the squadron was going to be going home to the States, and had a neat looking small motorcycle for sale for fifty bucks. He even brought it to my house. I thought I really had a good buy, but after the sale and he had gone I attempted to ride this vehicle. I sat down on the seat, with my feet on the ground and at that moment I realized that I did not have the strength to even balance or hold this machine. I was still in recovery mode, and the thought of just going down a bumpy road sent a message to my brain, "What have I done?"

Needless to say, I found another buyer before very long.

CHAPTER FIVE

Rehab, bull sessions, fixes, transfers, back to flying

After awhile the aches and the pain started to seem routine, verses normal activities, however they seem to be getting in the way every time I really wanted to do something, and could not do it. It was nice though to be home and know that when the night time came, that I would be in my own bed, even though I had a large board on my side, just under the sheet. There were also the push- ups and sit-ups, plus the rest of the exercises I was suppose to do. It was impossible for the first week or so, but I had to go through the motions anyway. It was the beginning of the third week that I actually picked myself up off of the floor during a push up, which even surprised me. All of the effort started to come together, and I was getting my hopes up of the thought that my back was healing.

In the mornings after I had the back up aircraft inspected, and it was roped off, I would stop by our squadron's coffee shop. There the war stories began. The flight engineers grouped to go over their latest updates on gossip mostly, but some education did come out of the "Bull sessions". Mechanical

Charles McCoy

brake downs and remedies or fixes were most of what the talks covered. Some questions like what would happen if the fuel got shut off to the engine, where would the RPM (Speed) of the prop go? The answer was about 40%, and that is where the negative torque system would normally take it so the prop feather motor then would take it on to "0"% during normal in-flight shut downs. This question could be proven on C 130A aircraft, by going to external fuel tanks that were capped off. Also later it was determined to be unsafe, and the engine and prop could de-couple.

One morning while there in the break room, Walter came in with a question that stumped all of us. It had just happened to his crew on their last flight. They were trying to get their engines running when number two engine would not rotate. They had checked everything, and found nothing, but still the engine would not turn. He even told us to think about it, and he would tell us the answer the next day.

After spending half the afternoon in the maintenance manual, I could only come up with nothing, I was looking forward to the next morning and I honestly thought it was a trick question.

Walter, next morning at the coffee shop said that after he had gone through all the systems that would make the engine turn; he said to himself well the only thing left was the starter button. After taking the starter button panel apart he found the ground wire broken going to the number two button. While starting that engine he turned the bleed air on to number two, off to number one engine, but hit both the engine start buttons at the same time and got rotation and start on number two engine. Then they were able to come on home, with only a starter button to replace later.

Our third daughter was born one morning, on 2nd Oct, and was a little jewel. Funny in a way, my wife and first two daughters were all born in

Oklahoma, and this third daughter being from Okinawa, well that made four "Okies"! That was ok for me though and I was just glad she was here.

There was one problem, and it was my back. I could not lift hardly any kind of weight, and even I did not trust myself to carry her or even pick her up. When I was sitting down, and she could be handed to me, then I could do my fatherly bonding and petting like fathers do.

Seems as though the flight line maintenance section soon realized that I did have a run-up and taxi license for the C130 and with some help from them, that I could help them out when there was no one on the flight line qualified to taxi, or check run the aircraft. This I did not mind doing, at least during the daylight. The problem came up when they tried getting me out in the middle of the night. If we had a departure at 0500 hour in the morning, I would have to be out at the back-up aircraft two hours before the first scheduled take-off. That made me there at 0300 hour. Then after I had my one back-up aircraft inspected, instead of me going for coffee, they would have sometimes two or three planes that required engine run test.

I did feel like I was carrying my own weightagain. Our on time take-off charts went to 100% on time. There were no missions aborted due to maintenance for the rest of my tour on the island. I did miss flying though.

Time slipped on and finally came the day I had to go to forecast for my new assignment to another base. When the orders came in, I was to report to Dyess AFB, Texas. That would still be fairly close to other family members that we could visit over the week- ends, so we were satisfied with our pick of bases.

Again, we had to get ready for the move, although half of our main items were already to be picked up. We had to keep our furniture that we had sent down here from Japan in a middle small room that we used as a storage

Charles McCoy

area since we got here. Housing supply would not let us turn in any of their furniture that had been in the house when we arrived.

There was also the task of shipping our car back, and we would keep the same one we brought over from the states. It looked like a new one anyway for I had gotten it painted and it was running great. I believe we had to turn it in three weeks before we were to leave ourselves. Again we had to get around the base during that time on the base bus. Then finally came the day for our departure, and a couple that was our friends and neighbors in Japan came and picked us up and took us to their house for dinner. They were now living at Kadena AFB, where we were to leave from. It had been right close to three years since we had first met them, and it was like having to leave family.

All the other couples we had met and knew from Japan that had been sent to Okinawa with us, we had already said our good byes the day before. Most of them had their assignment orders and some were coming to Dyess AFB too. Our friends that we were having the last lunch with were going to be sent to Forbes AFB, Kansas later.

At last after forty-one months in the Far East we were going home. We were going back with one more than we came with. Getting on board with a baby, and two little young ladies, we took up seats on both sides of the plane. We were blessed with well-mannered children, and they made the trip very pleasant.

Landing at Travis AFB, Calif., we took a bus down to pick up our car at the port where it had been unloaded from the ship that delivered it from Okinawa. It must have been sitting on top deck because it was filthy dirty, and oily. However, we loaded up our suitcases and our kids and off we went to the freeways. After spending forty-one months driving most of that time on the left side of the road, and all that time not going faster than thirty-five

Echoes of War

miles an hour, there was a problem. The traffic we were in averaged seventy-five miles an hour plus, and I kept going to the off ramps, then it would take me about fifteen minutes to find my way back to the freeway again. This happened about four times, when at last I realized I was giving out after the long aircraft ride across the Pacific. Finding a motel, we got showers, fed the girls, and then just passed out. The next morning while Wanda got the kids dressed, I went and got the car gassed, and washed, and bought a map. The station attendant showed me on the map where we were located, and we had only driven thirty-three miles from where we picked up our car. I had it figured we should have been several counties farther.

For the next few days we spent getting around to see all our folks, and letting them meet our new family member, and vise versa. Signing in at the base in Abilene, Texas, there was no housing available on base, or off. We checked in at a new mobile home sale lot, and had an offer that was great, and they rented us a fenced in corner lot, with climbing roses down the fence, and free sit up on a new mobile home. Just what the doctor ordered...Wrong, four days later here came the owner of the sales lot, and told us none of our credit references knew us, and if we could not come up with any credit approvals or references, in five days, we would have to move out of our new home. We had paid off every bill that we had after we had been overseas in the first year, so for the next twenty-nine months we had been debt free, and thought our records would still be there.

I remembered the last time we bought our car was in my wife's hometown, and the owner of the car lot was also the mayor of the town. I ask the mobile home sale owner if a letter from a mayor would do. He said, " Yes," so in a few days I received a nice long letter from the mayor, and also included was another letter from one of the salesmen who worked for the mayor. He

Charles McCoy

reported that he had known me for all my life, that I had good credit and good character, there would be no worry about me. That completed the sale. We got to keep our home, and were also thankful for our hometown friends.

After getting all set up, and checked into my new squadron, I was still caring the duty work code of a flight engineer, my new boss told me to go see the flight surgeon so I could start flying again. I did not think that I could pass the physical because of my back still hurting, and I could still not do very much at a time. I had come to the conclusion though, that it would be a lot easier to do the flight engineer's job, then to be running around the flight line doing so called "light duty" jobs. I told the Flight Surgeon that I wanted to try flight status again, and if it were too much, I'd ask to be reassigned. He signed me back to flying status.

I had to have three lesson plans signed off by an instructor engineer, then go to another base to attend flight simulator training for forty more hours in the cockpit of a room that looked like the insides of a C 130. To get the forty hours, it would go into three weeks, because of the scheduling into the simulator. This would just be the starting of being away from home again, that I would soon come to realize.

As soon as I got signed off and certified to fly again, I was assigned to a regular flight crew. How and why, I'll never know, but my new crew seems to be the only crew that was being scheduled to fly to Pope AFB, every Monday to Friday to work the test board, and that was to test the aircraft to drop anything they could come up with. One morning our mission was to drop some men out of the plane at 32,000 feet. This was to be done while everyone was sucking oxygen from a mask and the aircraft was depressurized. Even the men that were to jump had oxygen bottles strapped to their legs.

My Aircraft Commander asked their leader," How do you expect me to drop you on the drop-zone, when I can't even see it?" The Sergeant replied,

Echoes of War

"Get us within ten miles of the target, and we will glide the rest of the way to it!" For every four-foot they fell, they could glide one foot forward.

When we arrived at the one-minute warning, I got out of my seat and peeped around the wall that separated the flight deck from the cargo compartment. Our ramp and door was open, and these guys were already on their own oxygen bottles. When the green light came on, I could not believe my eyes. These guys were doing jack knifes, swan dives, and jumping out backwards. They called themselves Pathfinders, and they made their point in my book.

Every Monday, we were boring holes as the sun came up as we were headed back to our weekly job. Then come Friday evening, as the sun was going down, we would bring our landing gear up, and going back home. Normally it would be ten or eleven o'clock before we touched our wheels at home base. Then it would be about midnight, before getting to our house. This soon became a complete boar of a way to try to have a home life. Then one day I find out my Aircraft Commander had his own personal plane, and on the weekend he and his wife would fly around, just to have something to do. I just could not believe this guy, but he was a nice guy to work with. One Friday about noon we had finished our test drops for the week, and they told us to go home. We had filled our flight plan to fly at low level from Pope AFB, to Dyess, AFB. When we arrived in northwest Arkansas, the AC told the Co-Pilot to call in to change our flight plan to a higher altitude. Meanwhile we would fly around here at low level for a bit. The AC then told us he wanted to show us where his folks and his wife's folks lived. He pulled back on the throttles, reduced the airspeed, dropped the landing gear and flaps, and looked like we had a landing pattern set up to land in his father-in —law's dirt runway that was just to the left of the farm house. At about 100

Charles McCoy

feet above the rooftop, he added power, and we made a tight clockwise circle around the house. I suppose everybody in the house came out, because as we came back to the front of the house there was a bunch of people there and all of them were waving at us. The AC called for flaps to 50%, and gear up, while also going to max power with the throttles. Our airspeed had been at eighty-five knots during the circle, and now we are going up at 6000 feet a minute. It probably looked pretty cool.

One bright sunny day, while I was off behind our plane, taking a smoke break, and waiting for our load that we would be dropping to arrive, I was looking at this large trailer truck coming our way. It had a huge bulldozer on the trailer and it was stopping in front of our plane. Then it came to me that this monster was chained and tied down to air drop pallets, with cargo chutes installed, and this was our load, a 35,000 lb. D-6 Caterpillar bulldozer! This turned out to be the heaviest load to be drop tested on the C-130 up to this point of time. Our test was also to check out the dual rail system that was installed on the cargo floor, and to see if it worked like it was designed for.   I remember my AC asked the representative of the company, "What happens if it gets half way out and hangs up?" His reply was, "Bend over and kiss yourself goodbye!"

We lined up, using the overrun at the end of the runway, the AC held the brakes all the way down, until he had all four engines at max power, and I called "Power is good." The big bird you could feel was in a strain, and the engines were literally screaming as we started to pick up speed, but at a lot slower pace then we normally were use to. The far end of the runway was getting closer and closer, when it felt like we just floated into the air and off of that bumpy concrete. Our altitude was slow in coming, but the higher the better I remember thinking to myself.

Echoes of War

It took awhile for us to even reach our drop altitude, and to get lined up to our drop zone. Our chase plane stayed with us, which was a single engine plane, and had a photographer in the backseat taking movies of us even as we had started our take off roll. He was always there on all our test drops, and every one of them when we were done, we heard him say, "Hold her steady!" The first time we did not know what he meant, but about then he would shoot up in front of us, maybe a couple hundred feet ahead, going straight up and a few hundred miles an hour, scaring the hell out of us. After that, we came to expect the same, and every-time there he was.

All sorts of ideas were going through my head, and I wanted to see this load go out. By standing, and looking around the corner of the flight deck where I had often stood as we dropped our load, the thought came to me that right above me was an overhead hatch. If the load hung and we were going down tail first, could it be possible to blow that hatch and be able to go out of that hole with a chute, and what kind of chance would a person have next to four big propellers? Then I realized the company representative had a very good-point, and it made sense. ....Just pucker up!

The green light came on, the release of the drag chute deployed, and it was on a long strap that started pulling on another bigger chute, when the load started to move. Everything seemed to be happening in slow motion. As the load was about half way down the cargo compartment, the big chutes were opening, and our plane was slowing down. You could hear our engines getting louder as the AC was taking them to full power and our nose was in a forty five-degree angle. It was still moving, then all of a sudden we were clear and we were blasting upward like in a short field take off. After leveling out and throttles back, we all laughed when our chase pilot said over the radio, "Hold her steady!" As usual, up he popped.

65

CHAPTER SIX

Training and flying the new C-130E

Very shortly, in time I started to get use to flying again, and one day coming back home from being across country, the flight line looked like a war zone One of our C 130 airplane's wing tip lay real close to the ground, while the right main landing gear was folded up under the belly. A tornado had taken its revenge down the flight line, and made one heck of a mess, especially to this one plane. They brought in a team from Lockheed Aircraft to start the repair job. It consisted of laying down what looked like railroad tracks, (not drove into the ramp but just laying on it). Then with a large crane, they picked up the broken bird, and sat it upon a flat like railroad car. They were able to pull it to the end of their track line, which was about a block long. By picking the track behind the plane up and placing it back in front, and to continue this procedure on until, it allowed them to get the aircraft on into the hanger where they could work on it. The wings had to come off, so it sat in that building for about one year, or until they had a new set of wings made for it.

Charles McCoy

When the work was finished, it was my crew that would do the honor of the test hop. The before flight inspection went as normal as any test hop, or preflight inspection could possibly be. Every thing went so smooth; it felt like a brand new aircraft. Those factory mechanics sure must have known their stuff. About an hour later we landed with only a couple of write-ups on our radios.

My flight crew and I said our good buys for a while, because I had been picked to start NCO prep school the next day. Another flight engineer had been assigned to replace me while I was to take this training.

After I had my diploma, and reported back to my AC, and talking to him, he told me that our crew had also been the crew to take that plane back to the factory to get it inspected there. There was not one single write up on the flight down there, and it flew great. They had to wait until another crew came to pick them up the next day. Before that plane got there, one of the factory representatives walked up and told him, "You guys are about the luckiest son of a guns I've seen, and the wing bolts had never been torque down. Now all the bolt holes are elongated, and it will take another new set of wings that will have to be made." All the wing bolts were covered by removable panels and had been signed off by their company mechanics. It also was not a requirement to be checked before flight, except the cover panels had to be on.

We found out our squadron was to receive the new C-130E aircraft real soon, and all the flight crews would have to get qualified on them. There was a little classroom study, then on over to a base in Tennessee for more time in the flight simulator. Only this time, it was a brand new "Beast". I already had 90 hours logged into the old version C-130A, type and it was bolted to the floor. This new one had motion, and seemed to be alive, and real. All it took was 40 more hours inside of this mechanical class- room, with every conceivable

Echoes of War

malfunction being thrown at you faster than you could think.\My crew got all the way to the last final simulator class, and we had been very disappointed that our instructor pilot had not once turned the motion part into action. When we started to crank up, my pilot relayed this to the instructor pilot, and then we got our wish. He told us that he would let us just enjoy a normal flight, he would turn our motion on, and that he would not throw anything at us. "Enjoy!"

He threw a switch, and it was like real without having to fantasize anything. We had our sounds, noise, smells, and now even the bumps as we taxied down the taxi- way to get to the end of the runway. As soon as we got our clearance from the tower, we moved into take off position, and as brakes were released, power applied it was go all the way. As we reached the take off speed, the nose started to lift, and max power applied, the higher the nose got into the air. This was not right as I grabbed both the pilot's, and co-pilots headrests on their seat backs, and the only thing going through my mind was, "This damned thing won't roll!" I felt as if I was being sucked backward into the seat as we kept getting faster, and higher, and then our left wing started to drop, I'd swear we were pointed straight to the sky. Then there was a feeling we were going backward, tail first. A bright flash, with a god awful blast, then blackness, everything went dark, and silent. We probably had some funny looks when the instructor pilot turned the lights back on, and there we sat, with a what happened look that said, "But you said normal flight?" As we all turned and he read our minds, he said, " I lied, and don't ever believe you will have normal flights!" With just one flip of a switch, he had gave us a runaway elevator trim tab, which in turn made our elevator flight control move up, making our nose go up. Either pilot, or co-pilot could have stopped the tab by going to the elevator tab down position with their switch. So we "Crashed!"

Charles McCoy

Although we did qualify now on both C-130 A and E aircraft, we still had our old C-130As to fly in for the new "Es" had not arrived to our base yet. Also the other crews had to go through the same ordeal of cross training that my crew had gone through.

One bright sunny morning, another flight engineer had took ill, and I had to take his place going on a trip up to Alaska. Everything as expected, but just as we reached our take off speed, and started to rotate into the air, number three prop's RPM started to fluctuate, and the pilot called to feather number three. I hollowed out, "Don't feather, pitch lock it!" At the same time that prop speed smoothed out, and the AC ask me "What the heck are you talking about?" Then I realized what happened, and told him that would have been what we should have done if we had been in the new C-130E, had we attempted to feather, it could have resulted in a runaway prop and engine that could tear the engine from the plane. These guys I was with had not yet gone through the "E" school, but the AC told me to just remember that this flight was on an "A", and take my time.

I did check the prop fluid when we stopped to refuel, and there was no more trouble until we were on our last leg home, and number three started to fluctuate again. This time I told the AC, "Sir, it would be ok with me if we shut down number three!" He replied, "Thank you Sergeant." I could hear the rest of the crew laughing, and I knew my face was red. We came on home on the other three.

A few weeks had passed, and my crew got a Presidents flight to leave Dyess AFB, fly to Pueblo, Co, pick up President Kennedy's cars, and next day deliver them to Andrews AFB. This meant we would be paid Presidents flight pay for this trip.

Echoes of War

We were met on the flight line and loaded the big cars into our cargo section, and they were so long they took the whole flat section from end to end. One of the secret service agents asked me if we could lock up the plane. I chained up the crew entrance door and the right rear paratroop door from the inside, and put my padlock from my tool box on the hasp on the outside of the left paratroop door. The agent stood there with his hand out, and told me "Give me the key!" He also stationed an Air Policeman at the front and rear of the plane, all night long.

There was a crew bus that carried us on down town to a large hotel, and we stayed in the rooms that the President's party had just left. Upon arriving out front the large neon framed sign said, "Welcome Sisterhood Week", I told our load-master, "Man look at that sign, ain't that great!" Turned out a whole hotel full of "Nuns"!

When I told my wife, she had a good laugh and said we got what we deserved. It turned out that they left out the words of President Rates on our orders, so we got only regular pay for that trip.

My crew now operated as a training crew, and my AC had made Instructor Pilot. Our Navigator, and Load- master both were instructors in their field. Our Scanner was an ex-flight engineer from C-130B models, and I kept the training going to him, even though he said he was not interested in flying as engineer again.

We were called out to fly troops in and out of Mississippi, when James Meredith started to school. I was not for sure what I really thought about this deal, sense I had been born and raised in Alabama. As things came to pass, our crew ended up taking troops back out to their home base, and there was no problem with this.

Charles McCoy

The big deal came as in the form of what they called, "The Cuban Crises." We had not gone home yet, and now we were picking the same troops up, and taking them to Florida, land, refuel, load, fly, same thing over, and over, day after day. For twenty-eight days, before this mess finally came to an end, and we headed back home.

Our whole crew was awarded the Commendation Medal, and then I began to realize just what we had accomplished during that amount of time. The citation that came with the medal read, "Not only did this crew complete their 100% of training requirements, but they did an excess of 400%, while this mission was ongoing."

We also won the Crew of the Month Award, which was an honor, with some good letters that would help on promotion, and did.

Just a little while later, after we had returned home, and settled back into a normal life again, everything just seem to smooth out kind of nice, and enjoyable. Then one day I had come home for lunch, and started down my driveway in my car on my way back to work. Over the car's radio came, "President Kennedy has just been shot!" It was hard to believe that just a short time before that we had crossed paths, even though we had not really met, but we were family, and the nation was too, in grief.

After the period of national mourning had just began to get under way, and we had a brand new President, everything seem to be changing, but it was hard to put a finger on just anything specific. On television, the assassination investigation was on going, but it was more like a TV script, instead of real life.

The next month was December, and my squadron was sent to Okinawa for three months temporary duty. Being that I had just left from there just over a year ago. I was not too thrilled to go back. By leaving the first part of

Echoes of War

December, there was not enough time to even get a letter or a Christmas card back from the answering of my letters that I had mailed home. It turned out to be a very lonely holiday. The three months just dragged by, sense every place we flew into, I had already been there several times before.

Finally we were back home in Texas again, then a trip up to Alaska, but just overnight. Things were starting to heat up in the Far East, and with in just one month, it was back to Okinawa on TDY (Temp Duty) again.

Then in April, one night we left Naha AFB, Okinawa, with a plane load of Marines, including seventeen more C-130s also with Marines. The paper we had picked up at base operations had headlines that read "Marines to Vietnam to relieve the guards, so they can go fight the VC.

When we arrived over our destination, there was thick cloud cover, and our formation had to brake apart for weather penetration. I figured this is where all the former training comes in. Down into the dark soup we went, and so many minutes apart. All of a sudden we were just below the clouds and just above the ground. I have to say we were between it too, because there were mountains on each side of our wing tips, or so it seemed. We flew this valley for quite a long while and felt like we were flying in a darken tunnel. My plane was in the second nine-ship formation, and we were the second plane, making us the eleventh aircraft to fly down that valley in line.

The ground gunners had plenty of time to shoot, and even reload their weapons, which they did, we found out.

One of the eighteen aircraft took a line of small arms fire right down its middle. Another got hit in the leading edge of its right wing, and blowing a hot air duct into. By the time it made it to a parking spot, the sealant in the wings fuel tank had melted, and fuel started flowing from the wing, like from a waterfall. It was shut down with a fire truck standing by, and it was

Charles McCoy

not long before the left wing was nearly touching the ground, and the right wing pointed up like in a forty-five degree angle.

Our plane needed fuel, and I was operating the single point refueling panel, when I glanced up at the tail pipe on number three engine, and saw a dent in the clamp holding the pipe on the rear turbine section of the engine. After fueling, and climbing on a ladder, I found about a four inch hole had gone through the bottom of the wing. Upon taking the cover plate off of the dry bay section on top of the wing, and with a flashlight found a shell had missed the fuel shut off valve by a quarter of an inch. It stuck in a dimple next to a small crack in the top of the wing, and I had a souvenir. We were lucky compared to some of the other aircraft as for damage. No people got hurt on this mission but I understand the Marines secured thirteen miles around Danang AFB that day.

The crack was only about an inch and a half long, and I told our pilot that it should be ok until we got back to Naha air base. We all wanted to get away from this place, because there seemed to be a war going on with all these bullet-holes showing up in so many planes.

When we did arrive back at Naha, and upon checking the crack, it had grown to be six inches long. There was a fix put in place, with a large hunk of metal riveted under the tear. Then another crew had the honor to fly it back to the factory for a wing change.

Finally my squadron got to fly back home to Texas, and it was like going on a vacation. There is quite a big difference when flying in combat situations, and flying in routine flights. The aging factor from worry takes its toll.

All the exercises and drills to different places in the world seem to be running together. One week it's at Pope AFB, next we are at Sewart AFB, then down to Panama. It never really could be called routine, for something always popped up different.

Echoes of War

One night after leaving a base in Panama, we were about half way back to home base in Texas, when we had smoke in our cargo compartment. Cuba was somewhere off our right wing in the far distance. The thought did cross our minds that if we were on fire, could we make it to that island, and just how it would go over with everybody. Everything turned out ok, but we never figured from where the smoke had come from. We did not really want to see Cuba anyway, but we did come close.

One Sunday, on our way back from Pope AFB, it was a cloudy gray sky, with dark clouds far below us. The Loadmaster came over the inter-phone and said, "Does anyone else see something out past our left wing, which looks like a big ball?"

The whole crew was on it, and right away the AC said, "It's just a weather balloon." And it made sense, it was dark and round, so we continued to watch it for a while. After about fifteen minutes, with it still about in the same position, and distance from us, our Navigator told us, "There is just one thing wrong, Our ground speed is just under four hundred miles an hour, weather balloons don't go that fast!"

Well what ever it was, it stayed right there, off to our left wing, even when we went up or down a few hundred feet, for a good forty-five minutes. It was only when we were in the process of reporting it to ground control, did it just disappear. To us, we had our first encounter with a "UFO!"

For some reason, the Air Force sent down to the squadron, that the duty AFSCs of Flight Engineers had been changed from a 7 level to a 5 level. Well here I sat with a primary of a 7 level, but you also were required a duty 7 level to make Tech Sergeant. By reducing the 7 level duty down to the 5 level, a man could not be promoted with that on his record. The same day I read that order, I put in my papers to quit flying, and go back to the flight line

Charles McCoy

as a mechanic, where that AFSC required you to have the 7 level duty. I got my wish, and was taken off flying status. A couple of the other engineers told me that I was crazy, that they would still fly me as a Crew Chief. I replied to them that at least I could make another stripe.

Our brand new C-130Es started coming into our base, and right off the bat, I was put on one as Crew Chief. They assigned two Airmen Second Class mechanics to me, and all three of us accepted our new bird as "PET". We cleaned this machine inside and out. I taxied it down to the run area every morning, and got the different shop specialists to ride out with us to fine-tune the engines, props, and instrument panel. I believe that all the way from max reverse, to full power, there might have been maybe one or two hundred pounds of torque difference in all four engines. Everything was smooth, and really looked good.

One of my assistants came back from dinner one day with a couple of gallons of aluminum skin bright, and asked if he could polish the engine cowling. It sounded like a winner to me, and I was busy with some paperwork, and thought to myself that it would keep them occupied while I tried to correct this stack of records. When I did finish up, and came out of the crew door, they were just taking their stands away from the last of the four shiniest engines that I had ever seen. They looked brighter than a brand new silver dollar. I really bragged on their work, and the one who had found the skin bright asked me, "What about the leading edges of the wings and tail tomorrow?"

Well it did not stop just there, we all were rubbing on that plane for about a week, until it literally glowed, included the fuselage. The tail number was 63-7778, and it had it in large letters of just 778 on both sides up front, right behind and down from the cockpit windows. I had to take my wife out to see

Echoes of War

it and she even got in on coming up with the idea of a liquid vinyl cleaner for the cockpit floor area. I had to buy that myself, but it paid off.

The Wing Commander had been using the aircraft parked next to mine, and had even called that one his own because of it's tail number of 63-7777. After we had our plane sitting so close, and it nearly would blind you it was so shinny, he would come taxing back in after a while, and switch to mine. Then after a couple of trips, he made no bones about it, 7778 was his personal plane.

It had gone on a local flight one morning, and landed about two that afternoon. We got everything all cleaned up, and I climbed the ladder to tie down the right wing. When I started back down, I missed a rung, and gravity took over and I hit the cement like a ton of bricks. I knew this time that I was not superman, and that I had just messed up all the physical training that I had gone through in Okinawa, when I got hit by that landing gear door. The flight line expediter came by, and helped me into his truck where he carried me on up to the hospital.

After some x-rays, the Doctor gave me some papers to report into the Texas Rehabilitation Center, which happens to be downtown. Also some pretty strong painkillers. I also was assigned to quarters for about two weeks.

While I recuperated, from trying to fly on my own, and taking treatments on my back, that really seem to help, I thought I might be over my back problems this time. The rehab treatments went on for two months.

It was during this time period that one of the C-130s had crashed into the mountains in Formosa, all aboard killed. I was shocked when I found out the name of the Flight Engineer, for he had been on the front porch with another Engineer, about a year before, when I told them about my crew's near death experience with that same mountain range.

Charles McCoy

One evening a neighbor lady was talking to my wife in our kitchen when my wife, Wanda said, "I think I will get Chuck to take me out for dinner tonight."

Virginia came back with, "Just how do you do that, I can't get my husband to take me anywhere?"

Wanda told her, "Watch when he comes in and don't say a word, and see what he does."

After I came in and washed my face and hands came into the kitchen and in a few minutes asked. "What is for supper?"

Wanda, not saying anything, opened the freezer door, took out a frozen chicken, and dropped it on the table in front of me. She then took up the conversation with Virginia again about some things our girls were doing in school. About ten minutes later I said, "Why don't we go out for dinner?"

Virginia went ballistic with laughter, while Wanda was trying to get her to be quite. Too late, Virginia had to tell me, Wanda's little trick in order to eat out. When it was all out in the open, the fact that I did not like chicken, Wanda had used that same chicken for three years.After we all stopped laughing, I had to admit, I liked to eat out too!

CHAPTER SEVEN
New Job Title and Maydays again

My two assistant crew chiefs had taken real good care of our airplane while I was back and forth to the rehab center. I would run out to where it was parked, and check on them, just to see if there were any problems. Their attitude showed they took a lot of pride in this bird.

The line chief told me that he had entered my plane in a command wide contest for aircraft records. Since I could not get around too good on the flight line, I was able to go up to aircraft records section, check out all records on my plane, and go through, and check for mistakes, and matching work-codes to make sure they were correct. After two weeks, and double checks, I thought they were in pretty good shape, but they needed something to make them stand out.

The base had a service called Family Service, and they had a book published that they gave to all incoming personnel. They had a large color photograph of my aircraft on the front cover. The base photographer had made it right after we had it shinning like the sunlight. I got one and cut the

Charles McCoy

picture out, then glued it under the flap of the folder that carried the records. This way when the folder was opened, there was picture proof, and this was what I needed to make them take notice.

We won base award here and each base they were sent to, and finally at command level. At each stop along the way, there was a category "A" letter gave out to the crew chief, and signed by Generals, including the Tactical Air Commander himself.

It was during this period that I passed four years being here at this base, which we could put in for transfer to a base of choice. After talking it over with the wife we both agreed that Hawaii sounded nice, so I put in the request for transfer.

After two months of rehab, I was feeling like I had a new back, so back to flying as crew chief again. The Air Force came up with an idea of staging flight crews along a flight route from Abilene, Texas, to a base in Iran. Every time we stopped to refuel, there was a fresh flight crew to fly it to the next refueling, where there was another crew, so the only thing wrong was they kept the same crew chief through the whole mission. There and back, but I did get to sleep during the flight.

We were getting close to landing in Turkey, when the Co-Pilot went back to the "restroom", the loadmaster slipped into his seat, and the Pilot turned over the controls to let him fly the plane. What I did not know was this guy had a civilian multi engine rating as a pilot. I was sitting on the couch behind the Flight Engineer thinking this guy was pretty good. He asked if he could make the decent to final, and got the ok. The Co-Pilot came back up into the cockpit, and sat down besides me. This new stranger went through the decent, and lined up on the runway just like a pro, and this was what I kept thinking as he got an ok nod from the Pilot to land this baby.

Echoes of War

When we did get parked, and the engines shut down, the Flight Engineer turned around and ask, "What did you think of that landing?" He had a funny look when I replied, "It was a good landing, but I'm writing an operation hazard report on the whole crew!" None of them said anything else to me as they left. I never filled out the report anyway, since it was the best landing on the whole trip.

Suddenly, my plane had a little over 1000 hours of flight, and had to go back to the factory for some modifications. The flight crew prepared to start engines, and I had been told I would have a week off, that is as soon as the plane left. Number three engine started turning, but after about ten turns, it slowed down to a stop. Engine specialist came out and said the starter shaft had sheared, and the starter was changed.

It so happened that our line chief was riding with the flight line expeditor, and he said to me, "That's pretty good, just when you thought you could take off, your plane aborts it's flight."

I told him, "I think its darn good, that is the first late take-off logged for my aircraft, and it has over one thousand hours!"

With that the line chief told me he would write a letter of recommendation for me, and it went on top of the other "A" letters.

I did get about three days off before I had to take a flight of another crew chief on his plane. When the Flight Engineer showed up, he asks if I would do his outside walk around inspection for him. When I was looking at the crew entrance door, the closing mechanism was not in order, and the expeditor called the write up into maintenance for me. At about the same time the rest of the flight crew arrived. A little bit later the Chief of Maintenance came in the front door. He was a Colonel, and out ranked the pilot, who was a Captain, who just happens to have been in charge of our crew when I was an

Charles McCoy

Engineer.   The
Colonel pulled the door up and closed the door, and the linkage tightened up.
He said, "Looks ok to me," the Captain replied back, "We will take it sir."

I came unglued and yelled at the Captain, "Damned if it's alright with
me, and if you accept this aircraft, I'll never fly with you again!"

This came as a shock to everybody, including me, but I knew this door
was not right. The Colonel told me to prove myself, so I showed him what
the maintenance manual called for inspection limits. He still said it looked
good to him. The Captain said he would take it. I turned around and took
the book with me to a seat behind the wheel well, where I sat for engine starts,
taxi out and take off. I just knew I would be demoted since I had been rude
to the Captain, especially in front of the Colonel.

We were climbing to altitude when I saw a crack of daylight on the
forward side of the crew door. At the same time as I glanced back, there sat
one of the instructor engineers I had when I was at Ashiya AFB in Japan. I
went over to him and we greeted each other, and I ask him if this was right
when I showed him the book. He agreed with me.

I borrowed the inter-phone headset from the loadmaster, and told the
pilot, "We have an Instructor Engineer back here and he recommends we
put some chains on the front door." The Captain replied back, "Go ahead if
it makes you feel any better."

The Instructor Engineer gave me a hand getting into a parachute, and
also helped get a 10,000lb cargo strap around me and the other end snapped
to a tie down ring, with just enough to keep me inside the plane, in case the
door left us.

I had the first chain in place, from the top of the door down to another
tie down ring. I had the other one around a ladder ring in the cockpit, and

Echoes of War

just as I locked the device holding the chain to the bottom of the door, the door left the aircraft. At least it only went out about an inch, and with it all our pressurization. The door was making loud banging sounds, and the chains were singing as they held the door, and I was telling them in the cockpit, "We just lost the crew door!"

I made it back away from that area, and could hear all the talk coming from the flight crew as they were calling, "Mayday!" over and over, and the pilot to the Flight Engineer to go to depressurization.

We were a little ways out from England AFB, La. They came over with clearance to land there. When I got the chance, I told the pilot that we still had our door but only it was about an inch out in the wind, and the chains sang on.

After we were parked close to base operation building, the Flight Engineer released the chains, and the door fell to the ground. Everybody left the plane and there I stood outside looking at the door wondering just how I was going to get this heavy door back in place.

Then this guy in blue jeans and a "T" shirt walked up and ask me what had happened. I was still shook up and mad to, I told him from start to finish what had taken place. After I had it off my chest, he then introduced himself, giving me his name, and by the way, "I'm an FAA Inspector!"

I found out when we got back to Dyess AFB, that everything was all right when the Chief of Maintenance met our plane; he personally came up to me and grabbed my hand shaking it like we were brothers. He asked me, "How is your crew entrance door, Mac?" He did tell me he had been to my squadron to have my stripe, and that he had been wrong, and I could keep it. I told him also that that was the first time I had ever yelled at an officer. Even the Captain shook my hand.

Charles McCoy

A week went by, and I needed the Chief of Maintenance's signature for a work order to be able to buy some tools from downtown. He acted like he was really glad to see me, and gave me his highest priority he had to go on my paperwork, and I got the tools.

My new assignment orders came down early one morning, and I got what I had asked for, Hawaii. I could hardly wait to tell my wife, and it included concurrent travel. We would be leaving in January. Later, that same day, my squadron got their orders to transfer to Formosa, and only had a week to be there in place. I made a beeline to headquarters to find out if that cancelled my assignment. There, they told me it did not include me.

This was the first of December, so that when my squadron left a week later, I took on the job of flight line expeditor on the swing shift. When I got to work one evening at 3:00 PM, all the squadron's aircraft had already departed that same day.

Two weeks later word came back that five of them had been shot down in Vietnam. This was the time of year to be receiving and mailing out Christmas cards. We had already sent ours, and were looking forward to the card from Walter and Beverly. They usually wrote a few lines to let us know how they were doing. This time though it was just a letter from Beverly. Walter had been killed back in September. She told of the circumstances of what happened.

Their aircraft was to land at a base in Vietnam, and at the approach end of the runway there was the ocean. For some reason they landed short and in the water, and just did not make it to the runway. The water covered the aircraft, except the high tail of the rudder and the aircraft stayed together. The crew was the only ones aboard, and only Walter died. He did not drown, but had the long cord from the Co-Pilot's inter-phone that had snapped back and wrapped around his neck.

Echoes of War

As I read this letter, it seemed so unreal and I remember I carried it with me outside to the darken carport. Men are not suppose to cry, but I did, and at the same time I remembered back to that night in Japan, when he had came in all excited about the first crew to ditch a C-130.

Chapter Eight

Welcome to Hawaii, and to Politics

Sign out day came at last, and furniture already shipped, car packed and ready.

We had been at Dyess AFB, Texas for four years and seven months, and all that time we had not seen any snow. The Airmen had gone out and collected tumbleweeds, and tied them together, then painted them white and made "Snowmen" out of them and put them in their yards. We pulled out to start our trip to our new base and it began to snow. The weatherman was telling us to take a good look at the snow, because it would be the last we would see for the next three years, Hawaii, get ready.

There was not any on base housing available, when we arrived; we had to stay in a hotel until we could find a house off base. Our pay was compensated to pay the extra cost and we were right in the heart of Honolulu, which we enjoyed very much.

My new squadron had an old car that when a new man came in, they would let him buy it for fifty dollars, but when his car came in to port, he

Charles McCoy

sold it to the next new man, and so on down the line. This worked out great. I thought this was such a great deal and figured that it needed an oil change. When the service station attendant told me that it would take eighteen quarts I was shocked to find that the car was so old and it had a "Flush-a-matic Transmission", and the engine oil also drove the automatic transmission. At least that is what the attendant called it. The oil did not get changed that day.

Hotel living just was not a good place to be taking care of little ones, but the school was close enough that we could walk them to school.

My new squadron at Hickam AFB seems to be close on taking care of their family members and helped to make it very enjoyable as far as living conditions go. They would post on the bulletin board about off base rentals. Sense I was assigned to the swing shift at work; it made it nice that after we got the kids to school, and we could drive around to look at rent houses. After about thirty-eight days, we found a two-bedroom duplex that was brand new, and the price was very low. It was unbelievable and too good to be true. It still took a couple of days to get our furniture out of storage and delivered to our new home.

The movers brought our furniture in the morning, and we were still unpacking a few things and getting everything in place that evening. Suddenly there was this huge racket from outside. Next door to us were high grass, and a fence. It was used to keep all the pigs in that yard, and at about the same time we realized we were next door to a pig farm, the smell took over too. Just maybe, this was not such a good deal after all.

We just had to keep our windows closed and grin and bear it. We had signed a six-month lease, and housing was hard to find.

Echoes of War

My job on the flight line started to pay off. I was promoted from Staff Sergeant to Tech Sergeant and with minimum time in grade. They used the class A letters and the Commendation Medal I had received when I was at Dyess AFB. I also went from Assistant Flight Chief to Flight Chief, and had my own crew of seventeen men to oversee. With the increase in pay, we found us a better housing area, and out of the farming area.

My shift started at four and ended at midnight, and it was our job to meet the incoming aircraft, get them parked and serviced and do any maintenance that was needed. Also to take care of the flight crews as for transportation and anything that would help their stay.

Sometimes there would be some of my old buddies I use to work with fly in on my shift and it was really good to see them. It was something else to catch up on what was happening in their lives and what had happened to the rest of our gang. Sometimes sad, like in the case of Walter being killed, or for that matter, the list had gotten longer as the Vietnam War was still going on.

One evening when I got to work, after my two days off, one of my men told me that I had missed all the excitement the day before. He said that he was putting oil into a C 124 aircraft's engine, when he heard this strange noise that sounded like a lawnmower but it was getting louder and louder. When he looked up and over the wing, he saw an old B 26 just above the ground, at full throttle coming stright at him and fast. At the last minute it lifted its nose and went right over him and had to go higher to even clear the hangers on the flight line. Just as fast as it had appeared, it was gone out of sight on across the harbor.

After twenty minutes he said he had sort of settled down, he again heard this noise, but different and it had a miss like, "Putt, putt, putting, putt, putt,

Charles McCoy

putting, and so on. Then the same B 26 came into view, with one engine still going, and the other nearly torn off and there was wing damage. It would fly up a little, then fall down a little, up and down, and so on trying to get back to the runway at Honolulu airport, and at last he landed, with a police escort all the way to the ramp area. The story came out that a retired Airforce Major had drunk too much and decided to go flying again, so he had stolen this civilian converted old B 26. He had made the takeoff from the parking ramp, and hit a telephone pole when he made a turn a round when he had flown over Waipahu across Pearl Harbor west of Hickam Airbase.

I had never worked for anyone that was younger than me, not that it would have made any difference, but my boss now was a few years younger. He had made Technical Sergeant, with minimum time in grade, at the same time I got promoted to Tech; he had made Master Sergeant, again with minimum time in grade. He was one of the best bosses that I can remember, and knew how to get the job done.

I was picked for a new job, and it would be located at Honolulu Airport. It was like a white-collar job, for I traded in my Fatigue work cloths for class A summer uniforms. My Tool box into a flashlight and a clipboard, and I was now a Contract Inspector. There were four inspectors, all Tech Sergeants, one Master Sergeant and a Captain for bosses. The Master, and the Captain worked forty hours, off on weekends; the Tech Sergeants worked twenty-four on, seventy-two off.

Each of our shifts started at seven AM to seven the next day. Each Inspector gave the incoming Inspector the schedule for that days incoming flights of civilian aircraft that were under military contracts for the U.S. government. It was our jobs to keep the airlines honest. If they did not go by the contracts, and we wrote them up, they were subject to be fined. The fines would be determined as to how serious the offence was.

Echoes of War

We had to sign paperwork that stated we could not even accept a cup of coffee; much less any kind of a bribe, and punishment was jail time, from any of the airline personnel. We could buy them coffee, or cold drinks and the airline maintenance people knew it.

Seventy five percent of the passenger flights, and fifty percent of cargo flights that were under contracts had to be inspected on a monthly basic schedule, or we did not meet our quota, which proved to be no problem. If say one airline had four contract flights for any given month, which meant that three had to be inspected if all were passenger flights. If there were only two, then both had to be checked, in order to meet the quota, and so on. We always ended up above our quota.

Most all the different airline maintenance representatives were easy to get along with, and when we found any kind of problems, they seemed to bend over backward to get it fixed, to keep from getting written up and the company being fined. Of course there is always one bad apple in the bunch.

This one guy, the PanAm maintenance rep who met each of his planes gripping and swearing with each breath, was not a joy to be around. I never figured him out. However there was my job to get done.

One afternoon, this PanAm 707 passenger airliner landed from Vietnam, and brought in G I s for rest and recreation. It was to be serviced and taxied on over to Hickam AFB to pick up military and their dependants, and fly on to Calif. I met the aircraft, and discovered a fuel leak on the left wing. In fact the whole wing was dripping jet fuel. I informed the maintenance rep and he told me " No problem he would get it fixed." I completed my inspection, and had enough time to run home for dinner.

My house was now in base housing, and after dinner, I walked out to my car, and could see that the PanAm 707 already had been taxied to Hickam

91

Charles McCoy

air terminal to pick up its passengers, and still had two hours before take off time. It was only about three blocks from my house.

The last person the maintenance rep wanted to see was me. I went stright to the left wing, which was still dripping with fuel. He came walking up to me and told me he had wiped it down before taxing it over, and said it would be ok it was just a little leak.

I told him "No that it would have to be fixed before take off, and I could not go along with his decision."

He asked me "Do you have a civilian A&E license, and if you don't, you can't put a write up on my forms?"

I replied, "No I don't have an A&E license, but if you fly, you fly empty!" I then walked into passenger service, told them who I was and that I was pulling the passengers on that flight. They in turn got the Base Operations Officer involved, and he and I both met in front of the plane. He had no idea of what was going on, and the flight crew showed up about the same time. The Flight Engineer came over and asks me what was going on. When I explained to him about the A&E license, he told me "Maybe you don't but I sure do!" He got the aircraft record book and put it on a Red Cross. They had to replace the plane.

I really enjoyed my new job, and I had enough time between shifts that I could work at a part time job. I got on at a commissary, working for tips, and averaged out to be about two hundred every two weeks, which for my part time hours turned out about seven bucks an hour.

Working at Honolulu Airport, my travels between our office, and the parked planes took me right through the passenger terminal, where people were greeting each other, or were in the process of saying goodbye. There were a lot of home movie cameras clicking away for memories of Hawaii to

Echoes of War

be carried back home to relive their vacations or visits in years to come. I was working on flight schedules and had to get around them in order to meet my aircraft. I figured I might have some fun while doing my job. There was a commercial on TV that advertised Lark cigarettes, and they were always saying to the actor as he walked by, "Show us you're Larks!" Where they would pull out their packs and hold them toward the camera. Those happen to be the brand I smoked. Really I can't explain the urge, but there are probably over one hundred home movies that I was the unknown "Star." I was in more movies then maybe say John Wayne, or Roy Rogers?

Then one cloudy day, my boss, the Master Sergeant, called another inspector and myself into the office, said we had to talk. When he had our full attention he told us, "You two guys are going to have to back off this one Airline, because you don't know who you are messing with, and that is all I can say!" With that being the whole conversation, he walked out.

Tech Sergeant Cessna, the other inspector, and I just looked at each other for a couple of minutes. We both knew this one Airline was really in it for the money and they were cutting corners ever which way they thought they could get by with. Each time though it had turned out to be on our shifts that we had been the inspectors that had wrote them up, where they had to pay fines. I told Tech Sergeant Cessna that we really had no other choice, that if they were breaking the contracts, that was our job, to catch them and if we over looked the item, it could mean a life or death situation. I was not going to have something like that on my conscious, and if I found they did not go by the contract, I darn sure intended to keep them honest. We both agreed, and went on home.

It so happened the very next week, Tech Sergeant Cessna was the one to have to inspect this same Airline that maybe only had two or three flights a

Charles McCoy

month come through and he had to keep our quota up. It was on its way to Vietnam, and was breaking several of the contract items, and he put them down on the paperwork.

A couple days later, on my shift, I had the honor to inspect it on its way back to the States, and I too had no other choice to make sure we met our quota. I was in the front of the passenger section, and so far every thing looked good. As I started to walk through to the back of the plane, it occurred to me that the seats were only about six inches apart, and if anyone reclined, then everyone in that row would have to also. I started counting seats, and found there were twelve extra seats, and on a Pacific run, there and back, that would go into the thousands of extra dollars they were making on the sly. I figured this should be a pat on my back with the bosses.

Wrong again, it turned out to be a slap in the face instead. Not even a week went by, and both Tech Sergeant Cessna and I were called back into the office. The same boss said "I told you guys to back off that Airline, now you are relieved of duty, and both of you are to report back to Hickam AFB and back to work on the flight line."

I had to ask, "Just who were we messing with?"

The reply was, " Lady Bird Johnson owned the Airline!" The First Lady of the United States had just fired us.

Replaced right on the spot! It was really hard to digest that after signing all the paperwork that we swore to be honest, that our Contractor Supervisor was the one to be a crook. I could not help but wonder just how much his take was, and I figured his boss, the Captain was also on their payroll, and he was calling the shots. (In my opinion.)

I did receive an efficiency report as outstanding for that period of time I had worked there. The only problem, it was marked in one column, "Does not supervise."

Echoes of War

There was no way that I could be promoted to Master Sergeant with that marked that way. I contested the report. My grounds was that each of us inspectors was responsible for at least a few million dollars of Air Force Contracts, and it was our job to oversee the different maintenance jobs that were going on. If that was not supervising, then I had missed out on something along the way. It was pulled from my records.

CHAPTER NINE

Affirmative Action and "Operation 10,000"

Back to the flight line at Hickam AFB, and to a much heavier workday, or I should say work-night actually swing shift, from Four to Midnight, so it was about half and half. My crew consisted of seventeen men, just about the same crew I had before. All of them were exceptional good natured, and seem to enjoy their work. My supervisor was the same one that I had worked for, before I went to the International Airport, where I had gotten fired for doing my job. He agreed with me that I had a raw deal, but I could not go up the Chain of Command, and charge the First Lady of the USA with a crime.

After a couple of weeks, I started to get back into the maintenance game, and the sting of the Inspector's job seemed to disappear.

There seem to be just about every other day now, on my shift, we would be servicing air evacuation aircraft that would be caring bodies back, from Vietnam, or we would be taking care of aircraft carrying the wounded back to the mainland. Each time that we blocked that type

97

Charles McCoy

out from where they were parked, there was always a salute from the ground mechanic as the plane passed him by on the way out.

Our squadron had notice of the upcoming promotions, and how many and in which job they would give the stripes. My job code was for the turboprop field, and there was only one other man and myself who had this code, and one stripe was to be given for that code. I felt that I would get it and with minimum time in grade. I was counting on all the letters that were still in my records from the last promotion. Also this other man was just an assistant flight chief, on the graveyard shift, and was on the "Control Roster" pending to be busted in rank.

Two days before the promotion date, a letter came down from Headquarters, and a copy was placed on the bulletin board. It was called "Operation 10,000"! There was to be 10,000 blacks promoted to meet the racial quotas that had been set up. I suppose men on "Control Rosters" qualified too, because the other man, who happened to be black, got the stripe. Reverse discrimination was completely unheard of at this date and they called it "Affirmative Action." Many times sense, I have often wondered if just maybe it also had something to do with the Contract Inspection job that I had been fired from.

The space program was moving along now at a fast clip. The first flight to be close to another celestial body, was taking place. After the Astronauts, Frank Borman, James Lovell, Jr. and William A Anders, circled the moon, and then landed Apollo Vlll, in the Pacific. Then been put on an aircraft carrier, and flown on to Hickam AFB, this is where my crew met their plane and led them to their parking space. Next to where we parked them there was a stage, with worldwide television coverage in progress. We were making history.

Along about this same time period, something happened one night that was really odd. Another mechanic, S/Sgt Mitchell, and I had stopped on a taxiway waiting for an aircraft to land, that was running a little late, and we were to lead him in. It was a dark night with only a few stars against a black background. All of a sudden, Mitchell hollered out, "What is that?" He was looking straight out the windshield and pointing with his finger.

There it looked as if a star had came up from the ocean, and getting brighter as it cleared the horizon, then stopped abruptly. From the still bright glowing ball there spread a burgundy color that seem to just radiate out into the black night sky. Within just seconds the blackness had been consumed by this oddity, and then it was gone. We had no idea of what we had just witnessed.

The next day's paper said the French had set off an Atomic bomb the night before, somewhere down near New Zealand. Our only explanation to what we had seen in the night's sky was probably bounced off of the stratosphere back to the ocean, several times even before we saw it.

Charles McCoy

Right after this took place, S/Sgt Mitchell rotated back to the mainland, and the word was that he had gone blind. It makes you wonder!

Not even a month went by after the promotions were passed out, my shift was getting ready to take off from work, and I had the duty of giving the new Master Sergeant the work turnover. There were only two of my men that were still working, and so I drove the truck with him and two of his mechanics out to relieve my men. We got back to our office, and there sat the new Master Sergeant on the passenger side of the truck, sound asleep. I turned off the engine, and motioned my guys to be quite. I started once to go on home, but thought just maybe an emergency might come up, and could not do it. Better yet, while I was still in the office, our boss came in the door, so I told him where his new Master Sergeant was parked, but I did not say he was asleep. Nothing was ever said to me about this incident.

Another month had gone by, and we were about half way through out work shift, probably around eight PM. We got notice there had been an earthquake in South America and there was a Title-wave headed for these islands. It was our job to get the aircraft that was on the ground ready to fly, and had to be in the air in case the wave stayed as a threat of coming to our shores. That also meant that any aircraft that happen to land during this time to zero hour, would have to be serviced, and also returned to the skies. All of these planes were to take to the air at about the time the wave was to be arriving at the Big Island of Hawaii, and just circle.

Altogether, our shift serviced and turned around eighteen planes. At twenty-three forty-five hours, (that's eleven forty-five) the only two aircraft left on the base was an Australian Cargo plane, and Air force One, both had their flight crews on board and had their engines running. They were to take to the air if the word came from the Big Island that the wave had reached their location.

Echoes of War

Midnight, and shift change, my schedule board showed no inbound aircraft because we did not know how long this alert was to stay in place. I had two of my people at the two planes, that had engines running, which we picked up, and replaced by the grave shift personnel that worked for this new Master Sergeant. He let us out at the office. I told him the truth, there was no inbound aircraft that had been called into us, and that we had turned eighteen around on our shift. I just forgot to tell him where they were.

The big wave leveled out and did not affect our Islands. But the very next night at shift change, and the new Sergeant opened his mouth, a few choice words fell out of it. When he had calmed down I could make out something like "I had eighteen arrivals backed up from here to Honolulu runways!" I guess in my mind I wanted to make him work for my stripes that he was wearing on his sleeves.

A few weeks later, my tour here in the islands was nearly over, and I received my orders for transfer to Sewart AFB, Tenn. Now it would be back to C-130s again.

One bright sunny morning, and on my day off, my wife and I had the kids in our car going on a picnic to Bellows beach. We were on the main Pali highway that went up and curving and over the top of the mountains to the east coast side of the island. At about half way up this four-lane highway, we were in the left lane, when all of a sudden this motor scooter passed us on our right side. There was this guy wearing a dress and it was blowing in the wind, with his bare legs sticking out on each side of the machine. Even though he had a wig on his head, I knew who he was from work. At the same time my wife asked, "Did you see who that was?" She also knew his wife in our squadron. We both agreed that the wild Staff Sergeant did not make a pretty woman.

Charles McCoy

On to the picnic we went, laughing all the way.

Then the day came to ship our furniture and car, and process out of the base. A few nights in the base transit quarters, then to the plane back to California.

It just did not seem like very long ago, when we were boarding a plane and leaving Okinawa, but that was a little over seven years ago.

Again we arrived at Travis AFB, California, but this time in the winter season. Just coming from Hawaii, the cold weather was harsh to our suntanned bodies.

There was a bus trip down to the port to pick up our car, then we were on our way, but first we were going to enjoy a few days with our kinfolk.

About seven days later we signed into the transit quarters at Sewart AFB, Tenn. Only staying there for about three nights, while I was processing into my new Squadron, we found out later that the maids working at the transit quarters, had gotten into our suitcases, there was a jar of rare coins and a few other items missing from our luggage. I suppose we should have left the coin collection in our car, but now they were gone. I believe now that what had happened by that thief set a bad image in my mind as for me to enjoy being stationed there.

I was assigned to a flying squadron, and was the ranking Tech Sergeant, and had a Master Sergeant, and a Major in charge. There was another Tech Sergeant, in line of rank and with sixteen C-130s, the two of us each took eight of the aircraft, and divided the mechanics. We both ended up with two junior grade Tech Sergeants, and one ended up running my swing shift, the other on grave shift. For some strange reason, my shift as a flight chief took in from thirteen, to seventeen hours a day. The planes we had were just worn out, and I came down with the flu.

The hospital Doctors put me at home, sick and in quarters. My boss called me after three days, and told me if I could walk, to come on in to work. Half

Echoes of War

of my crew was also down with the flu. I could just barely stand on my feet, and even with the Doctor's excuse, I went back to work. Now thinking back, I probably gave the other half of my crew the flu.

We would get a new man in, but it seemed that in turn, we would loose two men. It came as a shock to me, when one morning this new man just arrived from my old squadron from Hawaii, was assigned to my crew. It was the same guy who was in the woman's dress that passed my wife and me on the freeway riding the motor scooter. It was not a surprise that he was now a single man, and his wife had caught up with him somewhere along the way. I never said anything to him about his ride on the island.

About two weeks later though, he was a little late for roll call, and when I talked to him later that he needed to be on time from now on, I had to add, "And by the way, take off your Mascara!" After I had gotten about twenty feet walking away from him, I could hardly hold in my laughter from seeing his expression on his face.

My long hours were due to the fact that only the other flight chief and myself were qualified to taxi and run engines. There were others in training, but right now, we were being called at all hours of the night to come up to check out the engines after maintenance or inspections were over.

There was one night the phase dock crew had towed this one aircraft to the last row on the flight line that needed to have its engines checked to full power. When I had the engines on speed on the right wing, I decided to start both number one and two at the same time, in order to speed things along. I got clearance from my ground crew, so I started both engines to rotate. It was then, out of the corner of my eyes I saw headlights come out of the taxiway and very slowly turn my way.

I just figured that the base operations officer had just caught me starting two engines at once, and was going to chew me out. There was nothing in writing that said you could not start two at the same time.

103

Charles McCoy

This car looked as if he was going to park besides our ground power equipment, for he was moving slow and was about three feet to the side of it. He did not stop, and was headed towards number one engine's prop as it had just come on speed. My right hand still had hold of the condition levers for both one and two engines. Automatically I pulled them as far, and as fast as they would travel, shutting down both engines at the same time, and in the nick of time. My wing leading edge lights, also my taxi lights were on, to illuminate a civilian convertible car, which barely missed the now stationary number one propeller, but now headed for the nose of the plane. I braced myself for an impact; at the same time I squeezed the mike button to tell the control tower about this unknown car that was going to hit us.

Somehow there was no bump, and out from under the nose area the car still moving slowly appeared, but headed for another aircraft parked to our right wing. From the black of night, three Air Police trucks, with red lights and sirens going full blasts, surrounded the car, one of the trucks had got between the car and the plane and the car stopped.

I still had to check out these engines, and the Air Police had this guy under control. I cranked both engines again, (one at a time!) pulled the run up checks, and then shut them down after they checked ok.

The flight line maintenance truck pulled up in front to get our thumbs up for the run checks. I asked the driver to take me over to where they had the car stopped. I wanted to get his name and rank in order to write up a hazard report.

The maintenance driver told me, "It wont do any good, he is a civilian, drunk, and looking for Highway 234!"

Right then and there I got the shakes, I told the driver, "Just take me to get a cup of coffee!"

Chapter Ten

Rotations and more Countries

The thought of just trying to get settled down into a regular job was completely out of the question. I found out that this squadron was in the process of rotations into Panama, and also into a rotation to England. Not to have enough to do, we were also to get brand new C130Es.

The other Tech Sergeant had been stationed here for quite awhile and had his feet planted pretty solid into politics of our squadron. It seems that because his wife could not drive a car, he needed to stay close to home. If any trips came up, and they were not too appealing, then it was the new Tech Sergeant (Me!) that was ordered to go. Even coming back from a twenty-nine day rotation from Panama on a Friday night, I was ordered to go back for another twenty nine-day rotation that was leaving the next Monday. The reason was this other Flight Chief had been on a fishing trip, and he was covered with Tick bites from his knees down. I had already forgotten just what was a fishing trip?

Charles McCoy

When I did get back to the base, and back to my Flight Chief duties, there was a meeting of Supervisors called my first day back to work. It seems that I was now in charge of all sixteen old aircraft that was to be transferred out. My Tick bite buddy was going to get the new planes, and keep all his troops. The eight aircraft that I had, and my guys, numbered only twelve men and right off the start, I lacked four mechanics to even put one man on per plane. The other crew more or less went on vacation, because the new planes were coming in to us at about one every fourth day

Murphy's Law said something like, "If you think this is bad, stick around, it gets worse!"

Our Chief of Maintenance Officer let it be known that he wanted all aircraft that we transferred out, was to go out on a black initial. That's saying there is not one thing wrong on this plane. It would also be a bold face lie. I had to learn how to be a salesman, and do a lot of talking, and learn how to lie legally. It was so bad that when I showed the accepting crew the maintenance book with the black initial, I let them see my fingers crossed. At the same time explained to them that our Chief of Maintenance did not really understand just what it stood for, and that he was also a. psychopath.

Out of sixteen aircraft, there were eleven to leave on a black initial. If they found anything to write up, we took care of it right on the spot. The other five crews more or less said there was no such aircraft, but did take some minor red diagonal write ups.

As I completed an engine run check at 0200 hours one morning, I was told that I was to go in for promotion tests at 0730 hours that same day. No excuses, and if I missed it, I could retest in six months.

I grabbed a couple hours sleep, and was in place at test time. They handed both tests and said I had forty-five minutes to complete them. I finished one,

Echoes of War

and started on the other one, but fell asleep and made a point five failing grade on the skill level. That nineteen-hour day had got to me.

Another trip back to Panama, in the summer heat, but it did seem to have a small shower of rain everyday, which I began to look forward to.

One of our C130s had gotten stuck in the mud in Paraguay. Our Maintenance Officer, who was a Captain, I, and a maintenance crew from Panama, were flown down with picks and shovels. Also we carried air compressors and air bag jacks. I was thinking this was a good time to see some of South America.

As soon as we arrived, they had a bus to take us to a hotel, and the Captain said we had a long day ahead of us tomorrow and to get some sleep. The hotel bragged on their free continental breakfast we could have in the morning. Their kitchen was now closed for the night.

The Captain was an early riser and one good thing the restaurant was now open when we got downstairs. It came as a shock when our breakfast was served.

Our coffee so strong the sugar would not sink, and was in a child's teacup. I had to have coffee to get me started. The waiter spoke no English, so I stood up and used my finger to get him to follow me. Everyone acted surprised when I led him through the door to the kitchen, where I found a real full size American looking cup. After I dumped my little cup into the big cup, and put my finger on the hot water tap, the waiter filled it the rest of the way up. Both of us just grinned, and I told him "Thanks!" I was the only one to have a good cup of coffee that day.

The bus ride out to the airfield gave us a picture of nothing but farmland, but it was being worked like I imagined it to be in the 1800s. We saw a lot of Donkeys. Also most of the women were walking around carrying huge items

Charles McCoy

on top of their heads. Arriving at the airfield, we could see the C130 very clear. Its Pilot had tried to make a turn a round on the narrow taxiway, when the right main landing gear hit a mud hole that reminded me of a large mud bath tub. The plane's belly around the wheels on that side was resting on the ground. The left wing jutted upward at nearly a forty-five degree angle. The right wing tip was even with my belt buckle. Both the large and small landing gear doors had damage, but that proved no problem.

We started three men digging around the back of the right wheel well area, and the other four started sitting up the air bag jacks that had been delivered sometimes in the night from the plane that brought us down here.

There was a D-6 Caterpillar bulldozer working on the runway, and I told the Captain, that we needed to borrow that machine. He told me that was a good idea, but went a step more, and he just disappeared for about an hour. The next time I saw him, he was in a large truck and trailer with two of the longest mahogany squared off logs I had ever seen. They had to have been 20 feet long, by 18 inches by12 inches. The Captain said they were used to let the bulldozer cross the runway and taxiway by driving on the wood. These boards were so hard that they also had no dents. The bulldozer was on its way to us.

The air compressor was doing its job on the air bag jacks, the size of the things were huge. The right wing had two sets of bags of one on top of the other, and the wing was coming up to nearly level with the left one. All of a sudden there was a loud bang as one of the bags blew out a very large hole. The gust of wind caught one of the guys that was standing too close and blew him off his feet for a good four feet, and rolled him on the ground. He did not get hurt, but scared the daylights out of him.

We were able to put another bag in place and did not lose too much time. We then got one of the large boards started under the right rear wheel. As the

Echoes of War

plane's wing was lifted higher and higher, we scooted the board on under the right front wheel. Our ditch that the board was in had to be extended on out in order to get the top of the board to be level and even to the ground. With the plane now resting on the board, we then started the pressure down on the bags. Hooking several 25,000 LB chains together we tied each tie down ring located on the back of each main gear strut to our borrowed bulldozer. With the flight crew in the cockpit to ride the brakes, the bulldozer driver started backing up slowly and the slack in the chains disappeared. Back came the C130 and up on to the taxiway as the pilot used nose gear steering to bypass the large hole. The bulldozer never got out of idle I don't think.

We loaded all our tools and tied them down in the center of the cargo section. Taking our seats, the crew started two engines and taxied the plane up in front of the passenger terminal where we parked. The flight crew had a case of beer they had onboard that they gave our maintenance crew for digging them out.

Our team Captain grabbed the garbage can and took off toward the terminal. The flight crew went to file its flight plan. I went into the terminal thinking there should be some food for sale in there.

Sure enough there was a snack bar, and I spotted a large plate of Impanados. They looked like fried apple pies, but had meat that taste like Tacos. I bought the whole platter and handed the lady a five-dollar bill. I ask her if that covered the ticket. She grinned and shook her head up and down. I did not get any change as she put them in a paper sack. We were both happy.

Back at the plane, I had time to take in the scenery, and right across from the terminal there sat an old Constellation that use to be the pride of the air. It was covered with dirt, and every tire was flat. It had been sitting there for years. We were told that its cargo was still on board and was considered

Charles McCoy

contraband items. The aircraft had brought in Televisions and they were outlawed items here.

About this time our Captain returned with the garbage can that had been washed and was now full of ice. I figured this guy can do anything, borrow bulldozers, get ice, there is just no telling! Of course our case of beer went into the can.

It was not very long before we were back in the plane and lifting the nose up in the air, and headed for Panama. I brought out the snacks, and our Captain handed out the beer. After I had ate one of these Taco tasting treats, I told the Sergeant sitting next to me that these things really went good with the cold beer.

He replied back, "Yea, if you like Iguana, you know that's what you are eating don't you?"

Well, that was what I had been eating. Thinking back now I think it really was beef.

My rotation at Panama seemed to be in a rut, until one morning I had the chance to fly out on a training mission going into Honduras. There were five C-130s, and a whole bunch of Army troops, with jeeps and equipment, that would be unloaded as soon as we landed there.

I had a seat on the couch in the cockpit, and had a headset on, and I guess I was reminiscing, and enjoying the flight. We were flying over jungle and the mountains were off to our right, and stright ahead. The blue and green Pacific waters and small islands in sight off our left wing completed the morning picture.

The silence ended when the pilot announced over the headsets, "Oh yea fellows, this is no war games, so stay away from windows and doors. There may be some shooting down there!"

Echoes of War

Ten minutes later we came over the mountain and into the view of our landing strip. There were barrels of oil on fire on both sides of the runway, and more smoke than you can imagine. Our planes were to land at one-minute intervals, between the smokes. Our rear upper loading door was open, and the truck loading ramps were already in place to release their tie-down straps, as soon as we were stopped. After our turn off from the runway, we made a fast taxi run onto a parking ramp, while at the same time the loading ramp was aligned to the main floor of the plane. The vehicles were released from their tie downs and their engines started.

The aircraft stopped, the ramp came down and truck-loading ramps dropped. In less than one minute, all troops and jeeps cleared the plane and the ramp was coming up. We were on the move, and headed back to the smoke. Another five minutes we were back in the air. I thought to myself, "Had I dreamed all of this, it was just too quick to even have felt real?"

It felt good to be landing back at Panama, and leaving that smoke filled airfield we had just left from. It brought back memories from 1964, when I had arrived at Danang AFB, South Vietnam.

Back to Sewart AFB, Tennessee, but only for a couple of weeks. Our squadron then had to go on a rotation to England that would be for three months.

After we arrived, our squadron now lived in an old two story barracks, but not too far from the chow hall. Open bays instead of rooms, and had probably been there before the end of World War Two.

There was a story going around that the aircraft parking spot number 15 was haunted. We had a few good laughs about that, and I thought that it was just made up in order to give this place some character.

I don't really believe in ghost, but I have no explanation, as to the events of one night and spot 15.

111

Charles McCoy

There were two of our mechanics at work on top of the right wing of one of our planes that was parked on spot 15. I had driven up to check on them, and see if they needed parts or help. As my truck's headlights shown upon the maintenance stand, I noticed the safety lock was hanging by its chain. I had to use its jack to get it up higher, in order to get the lock in place.

The stand was already at wing level where they had stepped on to the wing. I went up to check with them, and stayed on the stand's platform and chatted with them. One of the guys told me they would be another thirty minutes, and would I come back to get them.

I had left the truck engine running and the lights on shinning on the stand. A cold chill hit me as I sat down in the driver's seat, when my eyes focused on the safety lock dangling on the end of its chain. I got out and reinstalled the lock again.

I drove back to our maintenance office thinking that I just thought that I had put the lock in place the first time. My only problem was I also remembered letting the hydraulic pressure off both times, and the weight of the stand was on the locks. I did not feel any movement while I was on the stand. It just did not make sense.

I had no answer when I went back in thirty minutes to pick up the two men, and there the chain again was holding the lock stright down at the ground.

I had not said anything to them about the lock. They said on the ride back to the office, they did not know that I had even put the lock in place.

A few nights later something else strange happened on parking spot 15. One lone crew chief drove out there to work on his aircraft's forms. There was an MD-3 portable power unit parked off to the side of his plane. The drive motor would not work to get it close enough to the plane. As the crew chief

Echoes of War

was pulling the tow handle and was about ten feet from where he wanted the unit to be parked, he could hear someone walk up. About the same time he felt the unit get easier to pull as whoever was helping him began to push on the back of the unit.

He locked the front wheel in place, at the same time called out, and "Thanks for the help." There was no reply. Walking around to meet his helper, he was surprised, there was no one there. On the back of the power unit, there were two black oily handprints, where someone had been pushing on it.

After that we tried to park our aircraft on all the other spots, not that we believed in ghosts.

We had relieved a squadron from Forbes AFB when we arrived here at Mildenhall AFB, England about two week's back. They still had one of their C-130s that must have broken down, and had work going on with engine stands on both sides of number two engine. One day, I was driving past where they were parked, and all of a sudden I thought of Walter's number two engine question that no one could answer, and they were working on number two.

There were men on the stands, and men standing around, as I got out of my truck. I ask one guy if the crew chief was around, and he told me to check the cockpit.

As I walked up the steps and onto the flight deck, there were a few men there too. I ask, "Is the crew chief here?"

He was the one sitting in the engineer's seat, and claimed title.

I told him I was from the other squadron from across the field and would like to help if I could.

That's when he told me they could not get number two engine to turn, and they had replaced everything, including the starter, starter valve, and the bleed valve.

Charles McCoy

We were then interrupted by this Light Colonel, which was sitting in the navigator's chair. He grabbed me by my arm and asks, "Sergeant, do you see all these men who are working on this plane? They are specialist who has been trained to do their job, and just who do you think you are to come here and think you can fix their problem?"

I came to attention and replied back, "Sir I am from the squadron from Tennessee, and only wanted to help, so I'll get out of the way," At the same time I turned and started down the steps. I was at the bottom step when the Pilot, a 1st Lt. hollowed at me to stop!   I thought to myself that the Colonel had sent him and he was going to really chew me out.

He asks me, "Sergeant, do you have any idea of what we can do, to get this bird back in the air?"

I told him, "I do, but I don't think the Colonel likes me. If I'm right, and if every thing is back on the engine where it's suppose to be, I'll have that engine turning in ten minutes."

He told me to go ahead and check with specialist and he would take care of the Colonel.

With the help from the crew chief and about ten minutes later, the flight crew was sitting on the crew bus that was parked off to the side. We had an engine specialist out side to stand fireguard and the crew chief was in the co pilot's seat to read off the engine start checklist, to me as I sat down in the pilot's seat.

I told the fireguard to clear me on number one and number two engine, and number one should not turn, but it was to just be safe.

With an ok from the ground, I turned number two engine bleed valve switch to the on position, pushed the number two condition lever to run, then punched both one, and two starter buttons.

114

Echoes of War

At that time, the fireguard said, "Number two turning!"

As the engine came on speed, I glanced out at the crew bus, and for a split second, thought I saw my buddy Walter grinning from the back seat of the bus.

The 1st Lt. had been sitting in the navigator's chair all along watching and learning.

I told him, "He only had a bad starter switch, but he could get home by starting it like I had just done."

I got a big handshake and a thank you from him, then got back in my truck, and headed for the chow hall. In my mind, I could still picture Walter in the back of that bus, and from long ago, I recalled his funny giggle.

This trip to England finally came to an end, and back home to Sewart AFB, only to find the base was closing, and moving to Little Rock AFB, Arkansas. It was good to be home with the wife and kids, even if we were packing up and moving after only being at this base only one year to the day when we had moved in.

This had been quite a year, with all the travels, I missed my discharge and reenlistment date, also Christmas without my family. I had re-enlisted on the trip home in the air. I think I was actually a civilian for about a three-week period.

Where I really got mad was after I had my family moved into our new home at Little Rock, they sent me back to Sewart AFB, to help close it down. This occurred over a two- month period. I did get to come home a couple of week- ends.

After we finally did get all of our equipment and aircraft to our new base, I got the chance to give up my Flight Chief Job for the Flight-line Expeditor's. I never figured out if I had moved up or down on the totem pole.

Charles McCoy

We had rotating shifts and one early morning I had to start and run this one aircraft to check out the completion of a prop repair. Everything in place, I had clearance to start number three engine. At about 40% Rpm, the plane was shaking so badly, I aborted the start, and went to stop with the condition lever.

At that time my replacement was there and I briefed him as to the problem with the vibration and shut down. The prop specialist were there working and so I would see him the next day.

The next morning when I gave my turn over, my replacement told me he found what the problem was the day before. They had checked every thing on that engine, and could not find the fault. Then he told me that he then brought that engine up on speed, before he shut it down. He said the plane was literally bouncing off the ground, and he had never seen anything shake so badly. Then they checked the blade angle of all four blades on that prop. When the prop people had put it back together, they had one blade at one gear tooth off inside the prop housing.

I told him that I did not have the courage to have brought it to on speed, after the violent ride it gave me, nor was I that stupid. He just laughed.

CHAPTER ELEVEN

Changing Aircraft, going to War

Another trip to Panama for a two month TDY, (temp tour of duty) then back home to Little Rock AFB, just to get my gear ready to go back to England.

This particular trip to England just happened to cover the Fourth of July, and even though this country did not celebrate it as a holiday, they still brought in a sort of a fair group to liven up the Americans. There was even a very small Ferris wheel, hot dogs, popcorn, beer and soft drinks. All of this located right next to the NCO club, and just in the middle of a few tents, where you could win small prizes, there was a World War Two bomb shelter, which they turned into a tunnel of horrors.

The shelter was cement covered and was about thirty feet long, and had steps leading down into it from both ends. The covered top was ground level, but when you went down the steps, it was deep enough to stand up and walk through to the steps going up and out at the far end. There were candles on

Charles McCoy

the walls for lights to see by, and to see the Monster lying in a coffin you had to pass in order to get out.

A few days later and the fair had left the base, one of our guys found the coffin and rubber faced monster still in the tunnel. So for a few nights there would be like a funeral precession going through the barracks after lights out. At the front this one guy would be caring a candle in one hand while holding a bible in the other. A few steps back came six men and the coffin, and the monster would look as if he was waving as they went by. After a couple of nights the monster's rubber head was on a GI, who had taken its place and it was waving and talking too. Ever night there was something new.

Our First Sergeant had a time with the monster too. On his daily inspection tours of the barracks, he kept running into it where he was not expecting it to be. He might find it in a closet, or siting on the pot behind the doors in the latrines. Every time he found it, the monster looked like he was looking right directly at him, with his middle finger on one or both his hands, pointed stright up, at him!

He confessed to some of the NCOs, that he actually got a kick out of seeing the darn thing, and besides, it kept the younger guys out of the bars.

Not much had changed since I had left here in January that is except for the temperature. We were getting plenty of rain and fog. There was one foggy night, I was working the midnight shift, and had to drive over to the barracks to pick up a couple of mechanics and when we started back, the fog had moved in on us. We were in a large Chevy van and I had to slide the driver's door back to see the centerline of the road. It was taking us a long time to get back to work, when Job Control called on our radio to find out where we were. I radioed back, "I'm not for sure the fog is so thick, I think we are somewhere in Sherwood Forest."

Echoes of War

It took a minute for them to come back on the air, and then they were laughing.

Word came to us that back at Little Rock AFB, they had lost an aircraft in Eastern Arkansas. There had been an explosion and an engine had come off and had gone across the top of the wing just before it crashed. It had just come out of fuel cell repair before that fatal flight. Our report was the Chief of Maintenance had the Air Police to round up all of the fuel cell people, and put them in the base's jail.

My thoughts were that it was the same plane that had the prop blade one tooth off, and that was the reason for the crash. It was the next day before news came in that it was from another squadron, and it could not have been the same one.

It turned out that the aircraft had gone through a primary stall, which they reported that was the reason the engine had been shook off its wing.

I had the experience once when I was a Flight Engineer, an Instructor Pilot put us into a primary stall, to show his student what it would do. At first into a secondary stall, it would shake a little, then smooth out, before going into the primary, which was violent. I suppose if you were not expecting a stall, it would take a minute to recover the aircraft, but that might be too long.

When we finally got back to Little Rock AFB, and I started down the aircraft's steps, our Line Chief met me. He was grinning and handed me a set of orders for Vietnam.

I told him then that I had not been back from overseas long enough to have to go back over. That same thing I kept repeating while I processed out of the base. Nobody would listen to me. I also had to get my family moved out of base housing, with only two weeks to find a place to live, before I had

Charles McCoy

to sign out in order to go to an OV-10 school in Fla. At that time, just the word sounded Greek to me.

Out of two years of being back from an overseas assignment, I had really only been in the states seven months. The rest of the seventeen months I had been back and forth from England to Panama.

We were fortunate to find a nice three bedroom new house, and to get moved into it before I had to leave to go to school on this new plane. It was on Halloween night that I got on the greyhound bus, and going to Fla. somewhere just south of Jackson, Mississippi, some kids threw about a dozen eggs at the front of our bus. They were whipped like an instant meringue topping and covered nearly the whole windshield. The bus driver had to get down real low to be able to see through the bottom three or four inches of clean glass that was spared from the eggs. He did a great job of controlling the bus and getting to the side of the road in order to stop and clean the windshield.

I could not believe when I arrived at Fort Walton that my bags were not on the same bus. All my orders and clothes that I was to wear for the next month were in those bags. I took a cab on out to the Base and signed into the school Squadron, and next morning called the bus depot, where my bags had came in on a later bus.

Next day came and classes began for this OV-10 aircraft. It was equipped with two Turbo Props engines, and one prop went clockwise, while the other was counter clockwise. I came to the conclusion to just forget all my previous aircraft theories and start over, and it would make sense then.

This little jewel turned out to have a stinger. Even though it was a forward air support, this baby had M-60s on each side. It had bomb racks that could also carry rocket pods. Looked like a fighter design from the Old World War

Echoes of War

2s version of the P-38 aircraft. Its body made of fiberglass; light weights, carried a pilot, and observer, and could also carry three personnel in the back. By using pop up spoilers built into the top of the wings, it could do snap turns in excess of eight "Gs"

I kept thinking this baby would make a great crop-duster. I guess that I had been working on cargo and passenger aircraft so long that this fighter type craft was all a new thing to me. The instructors pushed our class through, but they made it interesting and enjoyable to be taking this training.

The last Friday night, while playing Bingo at the NCO Club, I just happen to win a deep freeze. One problem, I had come down here on a buss. I had to go home pick up my car, come back, and rent a trailer to carry the freezer back home. I suppose that since it was the only thing big that I had ever won was the reason that I just could not sell it.

After renting a small U Haul trailer, and picking up the freezer, I headed for home. This trip was hard to believe, for here I am leaving Florida and it was snowing like crazy. I had to drive slowly, just to see where I was going. What made it even worse was the fact I had to catch a plane to leave for a year, in just a couple of days.

Of all the luck, my departure for Vietnam happens to be on my birthday, some birthday present! I kissed my family goodbye, and I said that I would be back.

As our airliner had reached its cruse speed, the flight attendant came around and asks would we like some refreshments. I ask for a cup of coffee since it was only seven in the morning. The man across the aisles from me, ask, "Do you have Champaign, and if you do, I'll take that and his too?"

I laughed, and the attendant told him, "I'll bring you two, and more if you want them."

Charles McCoy

When we got to California, they had to help him off the plane. I thought to myself, "That should be me, I'm the one going to Vietnam, and besides, it's my birthday."

Boarding an American airliner DC 8, it was a longer trip going as a passenger then it was as a crewmember. I suppose as part of the flight crew it kept your mind busy. As a passenger though, my mind was busy. I kept thinking about the eighteen-ship formation when I first landed at Danang AFB, back in April 1964. From what I had been seeing on TV, and reading in the papers they were still shooting down there. This was December 5,1970.

Upon arriving again at Danang AFB, I felt like I was on a different planet. This base had really been built up since I was here before. Instead of one hanger now there were rows of smaller one aircraft concrete hangers with large steel doubled walls about four feet apart filled with dirt going on each side, and the back for protection.

There were now two runways, and taxiways, leading to parking spaces all around the area. There were several two story barracks, and one or two large buildings. A Post Exchange and even a base theatre with a chow hall close by. I was shocked that there was a Chinese restaurant, and it was only a block from my barracks.

Another Technical Sergeant, I'll just call George, that I had met while going to OV-10 school, was on the same plane and we ended up in the same barracks. We became good friends.

The first day we were issued our linen, and assigned to where we were to live and work. The second day, there were two large 6x6 trucks we had to get into the back, with about twenty more men who had came in to the base with us, and take a ride. We stopped at the squadron supply room, where they handed out each one of us an M-16 rifle. They told us we had to qualify on

Echoes of War

the M-16, Vietnamese style. Each man on those trucks had already qualified on the M-16, before we left the States.

The trucks took us right through the front gate, and proceeded right on through town. Finding a dirt road and going into the trees, but at the same time we were going up a mountain. It was named "Freedom Hill", where back in 1968 over two thousand of our men died taking it from the North.

Near the top of this hill, our trucks pulled off the road into a large flat area, I thought should have had a service station and snack bar; I guess I was just wishing. We were told to get out of the trucks, stay away from and don't shoot at any sandbags for there were booby traps next to them.

When one guy ask where were our targets, we were told if you can shoot the side of the hill, then you are qualified on the M-16, so have fun, you each have 100 rounds to play with before we go home.

So for the next ten or fifteen minutes, we made up our own sounds of war. I think each of us ended up going to rapid fire, just to get the feel of a machine gun. As our supply of rounds got fewer and fewer, it got quieter as the slower shooters were taking more time to play with this new toy. After a bit the last shots fired, we were told to get back on the trucks. There came a new kind of sound like a zing then a small pop, then dirt started flying, and bullets started hitting the side of the trucks. It was a rush getting all the guys back into the trucks, at the same time the trucks started moving and some of the last guys to board had to be hauled up by the other men. We came down the side of that hill a lot faster then we went up. No one got hit, but a few shins got scraped getting on the trucks. We were lucky, that those other guys did not qualify on their AK-47s.

When we got back to turn in our M-16s at our squadron supply we got a surprise. Even though our squadron of four hundred men was the largest Air

Charles McCoy

Force squadron in Vietnam, we only had twenty-eight M-16s to go around. That wasn't the worse part; they were all locked up in a large shipping crate. It made you wonder!

I had worked in an aircraft inspection dock before, so they assigned me to the OV-10 Phase dock. Our hanger had enough room to park two of them, one behind the other. There was a Tech Sergeant in charge that would be rotating back to the States in about three months. I had him beat in rank, but this aircraft was brand new to me, I ask him to just bear with me as he checked me out to take over his duties when he leaves. We had a good group of hard workingmen, and my main job ended up in the paperwork "office", and parts runner.

There were a lot of things done different on aircraft when you were in a war zone. One day I walked into my office and the other Tech had three anti collision lights all completely disassembled on my desk working on them. He was installing new brushes in the motors, using the lead from number two pencils. This kind of repair was supposed to be sent back to the factory, but he said they took too long, and without them the aircraft would have been grounded. Also the landing light would ground the plane if it were not installed, so we had to make sure we had about ten on hand. We had two very large wooden boxes we kept our cherished parts supply in, and when one was removed, we placed the order for another to take its place. It went into the box when it arrived.

One day while on a bus that was going to the chow hall, there was a Navy plane at the end of the runway getting ready for take-off. Our bus had just come around the end of the two runways, and we were about at the four thousand -foot marks of the runways. One guy on the bus hollered, "Look at that!"

124

Echoes of War

The Navy plane was screaming down the runway, while at the same time its left wing was coming up in a weird angle. The pilot was hanging under a parachute, back at the start of the runway. Then the aircraft dug in the ground as its two 500 pound bombs went sailing off toward the end of the runways. The word "Loud" is just not big enough to even begin to qualify to describe the sounds that those bombs made.

The mountain that we had qualified on the M-16s, "Freedom Hill", had a radar shack on the very top. It sort of became our beacon in the night. There were men up there every night, and they kept flares up in the air continuous to light up the darkness. From dusk to dawn it was assurance or maybe we could use the word insurance, but I know that we could see those flares from anywhere on the base.

As I had said before that there were barracks, but the majority of the troops lived in "houches". These were made up from tents, tin, and plywood, just whatever they could throw together. Some of them looked like they came from the book "Ala Baba and the Forty Thieves"; I'm talking nice! I was glad to have found my spot in the barracks. I felt even better when I tried to hang a picture of my wife on the wall next to my bunk, I could not drive a nail into the outside wall, and it seems to have been made from metal.

December 21st, I had been here sixteen days, and there had been our fighter jets land or taking off every fifteen minutes, twenty-four hours a day for sixteen days. This was a noisy place especially if you were trying to sleep. You did not go to sleep, you just passed out.   One of our OV-10 Pilots out on a mission, thought he saw a truck go under a tree. Knowing it was the bad guys; he was able to get his last smoke rocket on the spot where he had seen the truck. The F-4 Fighter pilot who was flying higher and part of his team, fired his last high explosive rocket at his smoked area. This act set off

Charles McCoy

the largest known act of secondary explosions known to mankind. That hill blew up for nine days, leaving only truck parts and a wartime junkyard. All of this was to have been shot into our base. Both of the Pilots received the "Distinguished Flying Cross"

The South Vietnam Government ended up giving every man in my squadron the Vietnamese Cross of Gallantry. I thought to myself that for sixteen days work, that was pretty nice.

Christmas day and everything seem to be quite and nice, and knowing the chow-hall was planning a big meal was something to look forward to. A friend and I decided to walk around the base and take pictures. We had both changed into civilian cloths, and it was the first time to wear something besides military gear since we got here.

It was beginning to feel a lot like Christmas as we walked up to the hospital's helicopters landing pad. It consisted of steel assault runway landing sections, and on three sides there were two that went at 45-degree angles in order to form a windblast protection area. The base fence bordered the backside and it was like a tennis court fence, only with barbed wire at the top. There was a guard tower about two hundred feet from where we were standing. On the other side of the fence, there was about five hundred feet of grassy mine field, before you got to the tree line. We started taking pictures when I realized there was gunfire over in those trees. I even told my buddy that someone must be rabbit hunting. I bearly had it out of my mouth, when three rounds hit the steel wind bearer, and both of us looked at each other and knowing that now we were the rabbits. At the same moment in time we both made a dive down on the ground and had the steel blast sections between the shooters and us. These sections we were hiding behind had very large holes, in order to make them lighter and stronger, and I just knew one of those bullets

Echoes of War

would come through one of those holes. Then I could only think that this was Christmas, and would not be a good day to die.

Lucky for us, the guard in the tower saw what was going on and had gotten us some help. There was an armored personnel carrier that had came from out of nowhere and right now had stopped about one foot from our feet. It sounded like a Mack truck. Then a GI behind an M-60 sitting on the top side, told us, "When I start firing, you guys keep down but crawl behind this thing then you can stand up and walk along side as we get out of this area," This was alright with us.

We could not thank these guys enough, and all the gunner said was "Merry Christmas!" As he drove away, my buddy said, "That just reminds me, there is suppose to be a big Christmas dinner in the chow hall, and I'm hungry!"

Walking back toward the chow hall, we got in line two blocks from the front door. It took two hours to get inside. The Sergeant who was on duty to take the money told us, "I'm sorry I'm not going to charge you guys. The entire crowd came in out of the jungle, and this is the first hot meal they have seen in three or four months. Besides, we are nearly out of food."

We had our Christmas dinner, which was a cup of coffee, and an orange that was all that they had left. The coffee did seem to drive away the memory of the M-60 and the sound it had made going off right above our heads earlier that day.

CHAPTER TWELVE

Welcome to Southeast Asia

I had been lucky as to finding a part time job at the base theater, after I got off my regular job from the flight line. I had to do something since I had not been paid as far back as last October. Here it was Christmas and I had no mail from home, but was expecting mail any day now. Ticket taker did not seem like a real job, but at $3.00 each movie, and I could work two movies a night, it paid for my eats, and smokes.

What I did not know was that my pay records were lost, and there was no money going to our hometown banking account back home. (In fact jumping ahead, we did not get paid for the first six months that I was in Vietnam.) At the same time they would not let my family stay in base housing, back at Little Rock AFB. That was the reason we bought a house, or paid down on a house before I left. At that time though we never thought that we would not get paid. We did have a small saving put back for emergencies but it was tough going.

Charles McCoy

Leaving the base theatre one night a bunch of guys was watching an Air Policeman with his dog who was "working" commands by voice. He would tell the dog, named "King" to do things, and he followed the commands. Like "Roll over, Sit up, Crawl, Get behind me." All of a sudden he said "King, King, Mouse, Mouse!" At that command the dog left the ground and landed in his arms, while at the same time looking around like he was scared to death of a little mouse. He gave us all a good laugh, and a good show.

The Air Policeman gave the crowd a little history on his dog-named King. He said that some of their assignments took them upon a hill that was named Monkey Mountain, because of all the monkeys in that area. King could tell the difference between the monkeys and man if they tried to sneak up on them. King would go into a low growl and place himself in between his trainer and the man or men. If it were the monkeys though, King would kind of whimper and try to get behind the trainer. The darn monkeys would throw rocks at King and he knew they would. He also told us that Danang Air Base always got rockets on the first Monday of every month, and had rocket attacks like that for the past twenty-seven months. The base was so large that if they hit one side you might not hear them if you were on the opposite side. Also if we watched the little white church that was just a little ways from the runways, and they were flying their flag, we would have a rocket attack that night. There had been times when the base sirens sounded, but so far we had not heard explosions very close by. Darkness would bring in a lot of noise between our F-4s taking off and landing, and what we called Big Bertha. Bertha was a very large movable gun that shook the earth when she fired her shell. The 50 Caliber Guns were pretty noisy but could not come close to Bertha. Most of the time we might not hear the shell when it hit its target.

It was just a day or two into January before my mail started to reach me. Then it would take a week each way for letters to travel. Even writing everyday, it did not mean we would get one everyday. Sometimes it would skip three or four days, but then I would get maybe three or four in a wad of mail. The letters kept me going, and we were still looking to get paid.

Then came the first Monday in February, and leaving work that afternoon I happen to look over to where the little white church stood. It always looked so peaceful and reminded me of the song about "The little Church in the wildwood." Only today there was a South Vietnam flag flying on a pole out front.

That night the base sirens went off, and kept up their warnings, and kept getting louder it seemed. There were then sounds of explosions and they were getting closer and closer, also the timing kept getting faster until it was like thunder rolling on the ground and coming straight at us. Some guys were yelling over and over "Incoming, Incoming!" Somehow not even thinking I was looking out from under my GI bunk when I started to wonder if the bunk was rocket proof. About the same time I'm sure there were four rockets landed on all four sides and less then a city block from me. My ears were ringing as loud as the base's sirens. When the rockets exploded, I could hear a loud crack, and the blast itself seem to me like it was an echo screaming. You did not have time really to think about being scared, even though I do remember saying out loud, "Not now, not now!"

The sound of the rockets started to get farther and farther away, and my thoughts of my flack jacket were on top of my wall locker. The locker was about five feet from my bunk. I crawled out from my "Hideout" and ran to my locker while I reached upon top and grabbed my flack jacket. At the same time I pulled the jacket off of the top of the locker, my steel helmet that was resting on top of the jacket, hit the floor behind me.

I knew that "rocket" had my name on it, as I jumped and climbed nearly to the top of that wall locker. I had a real good grip and I really did not feel

Charles McCoy

heavy at all. I just hung suspended in time, until I realized that the "rocket" was my helmet, and how silly I must have looked if anyone saw me.

There were a couple of barracks burning, and the makeshift basketball court was in shambles. The roof was at a forty-five degree angle.

Over on the flight line there were three C-130s parked behind each other. The middle one was ablaze and the left wing had been torn off from a rocket. While we stared in disbelief, someone in the front aircraft, and also someone in the rear aircraft were brave enough to get into the cockpits. Start the inboard engines and as the first plane taxied forward, the rear aircraft backed away far enough to be able to turn and taxi out of harms way.

The three planes had been in the process of being loaded with rockets in their cargo bays. The loading crews had finished the front aircraft, and were taking a coffee brake and were in a building a short distance away, No one there got hurt, as for as we were told. It would have been a different story if the front plane had gotten hit.

Those guys who moved those two planes should have received some medals for bravery.

This night seem to have been the beginning of the fire works that was to come. After that the rocket attacks were more often and more sever.

One oddity that came from this night of terror, one GI that had arrived that day just happen to be in the latrine and on the pot when the first rockets hit. A rocket hit the floor nearly between his legs, but did not go off. He was still sitting there looking at the rocket when they found him. They said he could not talk, but was in shock. He went home the next day, back to the USA.

The rockets that we were getting hit with, when they came down, and blew up, the explosion usually went out of the back of the rocket. If it came

Echoes of War

straight down and you were only twenty-five feet away and laying flat on the ground, you had a good chance of not getting hurt. The problem was if it had been launched at an angle; it could come in at an angle.

One such happening after an attack with an angle hit was really odd. The rocket slid down the roof of a building where there were six or seven security policemen asleep. When it came in about the same angle as the roof it just kept going on about forty feet away where it plowed into a dirt bank and went off.

It put about two hundred holes through the building, but not one of the men got hit.

Another rocket came through the helicopter hanger, and only the detonator blew up. All the lights in the hanger were hanging on pipes from the roof. All of the pipes snapped at the top and the light fixtures were lying on the hanger floor but the pipes were all pointing straight up.

I was shocked one morning when I arrived at work, and there was a bullet hole in the wall at the front end of our OV-10 phase dock. It also passed through the hallway, through the next wall and right on through my desk area, into the next wall.

The night before one of the weapons maintenance mechanics had pulled the M-60 guns for inspection and cleaning before the aircraft went to the wash rack. At least that was what he had signed off that he had done. After he installed the guns back on the plane, he had by past the safety switch in order to get power to the trigger switch. Standing on a box to the right of the open cockpit, he reached in and squeezed the trigger. The bullet he had not seen on inspection saw him as it tore through his left leg and end of his penis. He had been rushed to the hospital, and treated and was to leave out to the States that day.What I did not understand was why I was not notified,

Charles McCoy

After all I was the supervisor of the phase dock, and I was not even woke up. When I questioned the night personnel about it, they replied, "What could you have done?"

I did get one thing done, and that was to have a written order signed by the Maintenance Officer that the weapons supervisor had to sign off the paperwork on the gun's inspection, before being re-installed on the aircraft. After all I was the one in line of fire, if that ever happened again.

One fine morning I had a nice cup of coffee going, and was finally catching up on the paperwork of running a phase dock. In walked my boss, who was over both the OV-10, and the O-2 phase docks. He had with him the Maintenance Officer, and the Maintenance Supervisor, and even the First Sergeant. They wanted to know where our parts box was being kept, and they had to make sure it was hidden. We had PACAF inspectors coming into the base that day, and they claimed that heads would roll if they found our parts box. They took our supply box and strapped it across the hood of a jeep, and off they went.

The inspectors did come by that afternoon, but I figured they had only come to spend the night so as to collect "Combat Pay" for the month. They left the next day.

A week later I was called into the Maintenance office, where I was grilled as to why I had six aircraft on red crosses on the back-line. This was what I had been waiting for. When they finally calmed down I told them, " I could have all six planes off the grounding symbol within an hour, if they would just bring back my parts box that they ran off with a week ago!"

I actually got an apology, and about an hour later I got my parts box back. Going to the chow hall one day on the base bus I ran into an old friend I had not seen in a few years. He was flying as Flight Engineer on C 119s now, and

Echoes of War

he asks me had I seen his old plane that was sitting in the river down at the end of the runway. Only the left wing, engine, and cockpit were lying out of the water on the other side.

After I ask if he had been shot down, he told me. "No we were coming in to land, gear and flaps down, and lined up on the runway. Both engines quit, we ran out of gas!" At the last moment, they had tried to turn but instead the aircraft slid around and the tail section and right wing and engine went into the river.

There was one night when during a rocket attack, the north got a lucky hit for their side. The base's fuel storage tanks that had four or five large tanks around one in the center got hit, and you guessed it, the one in the center was on fire. It happened about two in the morning, and within forty-five minutes I understand the base fire department ran out of foam to fight the fire.

The next morning, it was still on fire and as large as it was at two am. The rumor was that a team from Japan was on their way, and with more foam.

The building where I worked was a good three blocks from the burning storage tank, but the fire was so large that we could feel the heat from it. I was surprised that the other tanks had not caught fire.

The team from Japan arrived around sixteen hundred hours (4 PM). The first thing they asked, "Were the other tanks shut-off valves closed?"

They were told that it was the first thing that had been done. However when they checked the valves, they were all wide open, and were feeding the fire.

The fire went out as soon as the last tank valve was closed.

We had a little excitement in Aircraft Maintenance Job Control center one afternoon. One of our squadron's aircraft O-2s called in that he was about ten minutes from the end of the runway, and he was loosing oil and oil pressure on his front engine.

Charles McCoy

Our squadron Commander and the Quality Control Officer just happen to be in the room. The question came up about shutting down the engine to keep from running it without oil. The Commander got on the mike and told the Pilot to shut down the front engine.

The Pilot came back with "I can't do that, this plane wont fly on one engine!"

The Quality Control Officer then told the Squadron Commander, "Oh yes, O-2s will fly all day on one engine."

The Squadron Commander then told the Pilot, "This is a direct order, and I'm ordering you to shut down that engine!"

"Yes Sir!" came back the reply.

In less than a minute another transmission came through loud and clear, "Mayday, Mayday, send out Jolly Green to my rescue, about two miles from the end of the runway, this plane is going straight down!"

The problem was that there were two types of O-2 aircraft assigned to our squadron. We had one type painted gray, which had loud speakers. The other type was carrying heavy armor plating and rocket pods, making it too heavy to fly on one engine. The Pilot made it out and back all right, however our Squadron Commander and Quality Control Officer did not come out smelling like a rose.

We were warned one afternoon that there was a good chance that the base was going to be hit by sappers this coming night, and that everyone should stay on their toes for anything out of the ordinary.

Everything seemed to be quite, but the warning was still sitting there in the silence as the darkness of the night engulfed what was left of the sundown's red glow. Nine o'clock, maybe who had dreamed up the sapper scare was just trying to keep everyone alert. Maybe just sit back and try not

Echoes of War

to think about sappers, or Vietnam, or any old war games. All you had to do was to close your eyes, and take a nap.

At about nine forty-five, one very loud blast, that even shook the barracks, and it had to be close. But that was it; no follow through, so it could not have been a rocket attack. Everybody now was wide awake, and wondering what was going on.

It was the next day before we had the news of what the explosion was.

The South Vietnam hospital was sitting right next to the fence that separated the base from the town. A South Vietnam Army trooper who had lost both legs, had talked his best friend into placing an explosive charge under his bed so he would not have to endure going through life with no legs. Only the bomb blew up, killing his friend, but since it was under the bed, it just lifted the bed into the air, and through the wall. He survived.

Along came March, and it was hard to imagine that finally my pay started going to the bank. I still did not get all of the six months that was due, but it was a start. At least we could make our house payment. Going to war is bad enough, but to have to go and your pay stops, well it's twice as bad.

April comes along, and now I have enough money, I can eat out at the Chinese restaurant (on base) a couple times a week. It was pretty nice and it had some of the Korean soldiers working part time as cooks. It was a welcome change.

We had the good fortune of trading whisky for cube steaks, or lobster tails to the Marines. When I wrote my Dad and told him I also said, "If we could only buy Bar BQ sauce, we would have it made."

A short time later I received in the mail a whole case of Bar BQ sauce. That meant that any time anyone in my squadron cooked steaks, and needed sauce my buddy and I was invited. Perks came in funny packages.

Charles McCoy

May, and bad news came through the Red Cross, my Dad had passed away. Before I had time to think, my squadron Commander handed me a thirty-day leave, and a ticket on a DC-8 leaving here at 1900 hours (7:00 PM) tonight.

I was the first to show and I had the pick of the seats. About fifteen minutes later trucks started rolling up and Army Troops started coming aboard. I know they were the happiest Troops I had seen in months. After all was on board and every seat was filled, one of the plane's lady stewardess came from the back of the plane walking up through the center and she had a can of air freshener spraying as she walked toward the front. At the same time the air quality became overbearing and they had yet to get some air conditioning going, and it was pretty warm.

One of the Troopers said it all when he said, "Its ok lady, if you had been at war out in the jungle, without a bath, for six months, you would stink too!"

The whole plane cheered with laughter, they were going home.

As the engines came on speed, and then the air conditioning turned on, everyone got real quite. Upon take-off, well that was different. Everyone broke out into a cheer, and we were going home.

CHAPTER THIRTEEN

Brief Stateside Emergency, then return to War

On a long flight home there is a lot of time to just sit there and think back to memories that were long time forgotten, or so you thought. Some memories were in color, but then there were the black and white memories that would more likely be placed in history books, if you were depending mainly upon total recall then the colored ones are actually the history makers.

So to separate the two, I suppose the colored memories were probably of the happiest moments. Case in point, the night you were introduced to your wife to be. Also in sequence, the wedding day, later when your children are born. The days when they first start school, and the day they graduate.

The black and white memories are the days you have to leave on a long journey and leave your loved ones behind, especially if it's destination is a war front. The same black matter applies if you are at a war front and you are on your way home to attend a funeral of a loved one.

I've flown across this Pacific Ocean back and forth, but I believe this trip to be the longest one yet. Upon arrival in the States, I got a hop from Los

Charles McCoy

Angeles to Nashville, Tenn. Only flew a little over four hours, but had to catch a bus from there to Birmingham. That bus was no express, and it took nine hours to go just a little over two hundred miles.

It was great to be back with my family even though this was a sad time. After the services were over, and getting back to our new house, I just had to keep busy, and I really did not want to think about my father's passing. I suppose I took it out on the largest tree in our back yard. It had a large hole in it near the ground and to me it might fall anytime. With just an ax, I worked on chopping that tree down for three days. Finally, when it hit the ground, a neighbor who lived five houses down from me, came running out of his house to see what all the noise was.

Another neighbor from up the street brought a chain saw down and cut it up so I could haul it off, in a large rented truck.

Oh, but it was good to be home, and the war was fading fast as a memory could go. There was so much to get done around our new house. I had not had time when we had moved into it, before I had to leave to go to the school for the OV 10 training prior to Vietnam.

Our three girls were all on softball teams, and were playing at the same time at three different fields nearly every time they played. This would prove to be quite a task.I told the girls to keep track of the balls they hit, and when I come back home in December, I'd pay up. Twenty-five cents to first base, fifty cents to second, seventy-five to third, and one dollar for home runs.

All of a sudden the thirty-day emergency leave was just about over, and I was faced with having to go back to the war. Of all things to think about was the poison ivy in our back yard. By pulling it up with my bare hands, maybe I'd be so broke out, that I would not have to go. I didn't even get a pimple!

Again, here I was strapped into a passenger seat going down the runway for take off. My thoughts were, "I'm getting too old for this crap!"

Echoes of War

About thirty-eight hours later, I was back on the runway at Danang AFB, Vietnam. For some reason or another, I had not slept a wink during the whole trip back. I had sat there and the thought of my father's passing, I remembered about everything he had done, or what we had talked about through the years. He gave his signature on paper when I got into the Air Force, and again when I got married.

Signing back in for duty, I did not have to be back to work until the next day, and found out I was going to the grave shift, and out of the inspection dock, and into the job control section. This was great news because I could not sleep at night, for all the noise from planes taking off, or landing. I only lived about four blocks from the runways. Plus all the noise from all the rockets, and big guns, which seem to be quieter by day.

When I did report to duty, I still had not had any sleep, and it was taking its toll. My new boss had someone to drive me to the base hospital when my shift was over the next morning. I could not see a doctor, but his assistant (PA) gave me a pill, and told me to tell my boss that I would not be coming in to work my next shift. I did and as soon as I took that pill and lay down, I was out for twenty-four hours.

My new job would start at 11 PM, and go to 7AM, with one day off a week. Also I found out that I was still employed at the base theatre, but instead of just tearing tickets, I became the day manager, and it worked out perfect.

So, I got off work at 7:00AM, and I had three hours till the first movie started at 10: OO AM... Another movie at 1:00 PM, then I was through at 3:00PM. I would go get a shower, then put the fan on over my bunk, enjoy one cold can of beer, and then just pass out until 9:00PM. This would give me two hours to grab a bite to eat, before going back to my Air Force job. Then it would go to replay.

Charles McCoy

Sitting on the barrack's step and waiting for my ride to work one night, I could catch up on what was happening in this war.

There was a small building probably about seventy-five feet from where I was sitting. It had a bench on the side I was looking at, which was in total darkness; although I knew from daytime it was there. All of a sudden, there was a cigarette lighter flipped by someone sitting in the dark to light a smoke. The fire from the cigarette burned a bright orange, and then it made a low arch and moved to the right. Another drag from someone else made it flair up to the orange color again. Again the low arch and it moved to the next person. There were five people on that bench and all were enjoying the same smoke. Through the quite of the night, I heard giggling, but after that sequence of events happened again, it turned into laughter. Then later, after the lighter had lit a couple more smokes, I swear those guys were laughing so hard they were rolling on the ground.

Another night I observed a fire fight between a helicopter (ours) and a boat. There were many bullets going up and down and it was over in minutes because the boat blew up with a huge blast, and I was surprised that the sound took about thirty seconds to get to where I sat.

I forget just what date it happened, but waiting for my ride one night I had gotten there on the steps about an hour early because of all the noise, that was keeping me awake. I could see a small village just a little ways from the base, and it was being shelled and looked like the whole town was burning. The shelling just came faster and the blast got larger and faster. I had seen fireworks being set off on holidays in the States, but this far exceeded anything I ever saw. This kept up for forty-five minutes, and I can't imagine anyone getting out alive.

After a few days, and getting into a sort of a rut, time once again started just to slow down, but we had all these rockets coming in to keep us alert. There is just no fun, when you are at war.

Echoes of War

July 4th, 1971, and starting in the morning there were warnings that we would be hit hard and it would began at sundown. The off base chapel had its flag flying in the wind, so we knew the warnings were just not rumors.

I was on schedule when my ride came to take me to work that night at eleven PM. Part of my turnover briefing was about the C 119 gunship that was flying low and going round and round the base like it was looking for something. It was and found three rocket launchers at 23:45 hours (11:45 PM). The crew had to call into headquarters for permission to fire, and until it was given, they just kept circling. The clock kept going and at 0030 hour, the 5th July, the rockets fired off into the air, and then found their targets in Gunfighter village. (Where I lived.) Several buildings were on fire, and we were told the next day that eighty-five men were being sent home and they were all missing two of their limbs.

The gunship never got permission, and everyone's question was, "What kind of War Games were we playing?"

The clean up began, and it was a bloody mess, and we were not told the number of dead.

One tail came out that a Captain had snapped his camera and flash at a Tech Sergeant as he was crawling through the window from a burning barracks. Then helped the man on out and to the ground. Once out of danger, the Sergeant politely knocked the Captain on his butt.

The Captain pressed charges, but when it came up at the Court Marshall and what had happened, it was the Captain who got the reprimand, and promise of no more promotions while in service.

It was into the third day of clean up, when the last body was found under a slab of concrete that had been used as a protection in front of a barracks door.

Charles McCoy

Gunfighter village looked like a tornado had gone through it. I was just thankful that I had been at work, and about a half mile away.

I began to notice a kind of pattern starting to appear from out of nowhere. It seemed to me that when everything started to quiet down, and you started feeling like a human being, then that is when re-runs from hell would be looking you right in your face.

The sounds from the 155 Howitzers were getting louder, and more intense. Explosions could be heard throughout the night. Night flairs lit up some areas most all night long.

My friend that had been sent to Quain Tri called me and said he was on his way back to Danang, and could I find him a place to bunk?

There was no problem there. When he showed up he stuck his head through the curtain that was strung between two wall lockers, which was our doorway and asked, "Where do I bunk?

It was good to shake his hand again for we had met each other in Florida when we were going to school before this Far East trip.

I pointed to the other side of the cubicle and said, "Right there!" I already had his bunk made up, and clean sheets and blankets. One wall locker held pots and pans, and even a hot plate.

He was the same age as me, but I knew he had gotten a Chefs license when he was nineteen years old. He settled right in and acted well pleased.

We started stocking up on food items, and the other guys in the barracks could not resist the aromas. It was not long before they started to bring in goodies to be cooked, and we ended up with about five people added to our dinner table.

After George (my buddy) was back at Danang, he told me about when he was at Quang Tri; he bought a jeep from this T/Sgt from our squadron for

Echoes of War

$75.00. They took the serial number from another jeep, painted it on "his" jeep, and then reported the gas card lost so they could end up with a way to get gas for both vehicles.

No one in our squadron actually knew what job that this T/Sgt had or did, but if you needed anything; you had to go through him.

A week before George left to come back to Danang, someone stole his jeep. He was heartsick, and had gotten use to having transportation to get around in.

He and I were walking to the BX one day, and he spotted "his" jeep just as another man started to get into it. So he asks the man just where he got it.

This guy grinned, and said from a T/Sgt in our squadron.

George asked him, "Did it cost you $75.00?"

The answer was, "Yes."

All George could do was just stand there and laugh, then he let us all in on the situation. He also said he had got his moneys worth, and the guy drove off.

We had all the transportation we needed anyway.

Chapter Fourteen

Storms, War, and R&R

The days were coming into September, and it was warm and humid and with my work hours, the only way I could sleep was by putting my fan right at the top of my bunk so the breeze could not only cool, but help keep the mosquitoes off of me.

There was talk of a typhoon, and it was headed our way. I figured that it might just be cooler if we could get some rain, even if the winds did blow over seventy-five miles an hour, at the time it sounded pretty good, it might also keep the rockets at a minimum.

The typhoon did not turn out to be just talk; it was real and bearing down right on top of Danang AFB. There was a lot of work involved, like having to move all the aircraft to safety. Our OV-10s were towed into the concrete covered revetments, and one end was protected by the double steel wall that had dirt between each side. Our O-2s were taken into a couple of just regular type hangers, and the large doors were pulled closed. The winds were not expected to reach typhoon strength anyway.

Charles McCoy

Wrong!

The barracks where I lived held up really well, but the guys who lived in the homemade "Hooches", they had to come into the stronger buildings for safety. Everything was being blown down or away when you got brave enough to look out of the windows.

We had the high winds for a couple of days, and long enough that we ran out of beer that had been giving us a cooling effect.

When the winds finally started to calm down, and we could go outside, it was a shock to see so much damage. It was really worse than a rocket attack. Down on the flight line, the OV-10s were ok, but the O-2s took the pounding. The large hanger doors had broken loose at their bottom tracks, and they had swung back and forth. When they swung into the hanger, the door would catch an O-2, and drag it back into the other door and literally cut a wing off, or a tail section into. That plane would then catch part of another and drag it up to be cut to pieces and it just multiplied to a total of about nine planes.

Our squadron went to maximum work hours, and we started taking wings off one plane or other parts and assembling them to less damaged aircraft. If I remember I think the total destroyed came up to five. I think they were marked up on paper as lost in combat.

When the storm was over, I had it figured that I would as soon fight the heat, and bugs than go through a typhoon again, but at any rate we could at least buy beer, but not during a typhoon. .

Things started to get back to a routine again, and finally got a day off. Both George and I had food on the brain, and just about anything we could scrape up went into a cooking pot, and George had the magic touch. He could turn it into the finest meal and he just called it "Combat Cuisine!"

Echoes of War

We noticed an OV-10 flying around the base several passes, but his nose gear was hanging at the wrong angle, and was turned sideways from where it was suppose to be. They had a fire truck foaming down the runway, when everything the pilot tried did not help.

The pilot did a good job setting the plane straight down the middle of some pretty slick gooey looking stuff. He kept the nose up as long as it would still fly and his speed gave away before the tire touched the pavement. He shut both engines down, but he was coming to the end of where the foam stopped. Then the tail of the plane just came around and he began to be rolling backward but slowed down to a stop. He saved the plane for another day.

One bright moonlit night, we had an OV-10 down on the run-up pad and there were three engine specialists trouble shooting one of its engines. They had portable lights set up, which made them perfect targets. Around 0200am, they called in to us that they were being fired on and it was coming from the middle of the river that was directly behind them.

We called in security, which in turn sent out a helicopter with a large bright light. In just a short time they had this guy standing with his arms raised in the air, and about in the middle of the river. The river was about one hundred fifty feet wide and waist deep.

A couple guys repelled down from the helicopter and came within a few feet from this sniper. While one of the security personnel stood holding an M 16 on this shooter, the other man started walking circles around them. Each time around he got farther from them. After the forth circle, he stopped and reached down into the water where he picked up an AK-47 rifle.

All this was happening just right outside our door where we worked, and our whole crew was seeing it like they say, "Live in person!"

Charles McCoy

The two security police marched this guy over to the bank of the river where they turned him over to the South Vietnam Troops.

I forgot to mention this sniper wore black PJ cloths, so after they walked him around the corner of the first building there was the sound of one lone rifle shot.

That was the way they handled Viet-Cong, and if he had been in uniform from the north, he would have been kept as a prisoner of war and sent south to a camp.

This came to be proven one day when a group of North Vietnam Army prisoners came through the base, and were being transferred south from one plane to another.

I asked one of their guards why they kept their hands tied like that. These people were just kids, boys and girls around thirteen or fourteen years old.

The guard said, "If they were untied, they would kill you in a minute!"

It was about this time that the US Army turned over their 155 Howitzers to the South Vietnamese troops. It took them exactly two weeks before the guns were turned 180 degrees, and they put about ten shells down between the runways one night.

I was going to pick up a couple of maintenance men, and in a jeep when all the fireworks began. The road I was on was about 500feet from one of the runways. You could hear the shells when they fired and a loud whirling noise as they came over. As they hit the ground the blasts were so loud and ground shaking it was almost unbelievable.

I don't remember when I stopped the jeep, or getting on the ground, but I can say I know what dirt taste like. It made you wonder just whose side "Who" was on.

Up to this point I thought that I would just skip my R&R (Rest and recuperation) but this night changed my mind. I felt like I have to get away

Echoes of War

from all this noise and I think I could sleep the whole week. A week in Formosa might do the trick, so I put in the paper work.

Only a few days later, and the plane I was on sat down in Taipei, Formosa. We were all herded into one large room where we listened to about five sales pitches from five different hotel representatives. Each was offering more and better things if we would stay at their hotel.

I chose this one called the Bangkok which had nice rates, plus they gave you a nice attaché case, dinner one night at the hotel, one dinner at a Mongolian Bar BQ restaurant, a book of thirty free drinks at the hotel's bar, and a six hour bus tour of the island.

After checking into that hotel, and getting to my room, it just did not make any sense as to how they could rent this nice a room for a week that cheap. I had pulled off my shirt and just lay back across my bed when there was a knock on my door.

It was the salesman from the airport and he was standing there grinning when I opened the door. Behind him there were at least ten young ladies, he wanted me to choose one to help pass off these coming lonely nights.

I explained to him, that it was not going to be, that I was a happy married man and I was going home in a little over one month. I heard one of the girls say in broken English, "Maybe he funny!"

Their cheap hotel rates and gift packages were not the money makers in this establishment. Two or three times during that week, the representative I would see or pass in the hall would ask, "You sure you not change your mind?"

It was good to just sleep in and get out of bed whenever you wanted to. Shower, shave, brush my teeth, get dressed and go down stairs for a good breakfast. Then I would take off walking and sight seeing, and doing a little

Charles McCoy

shopping. After about six blocks, I came to an American Navy Base, where I ate lunch and sat and drank coffee for about an hour. Rested up, I would cross the street and head down the other side, window shopping while going back to the hotel. There I had one Grand-dad seven drink, then a quick afternoon nap. Get back down stairs for supper, and eat so much I could hardly move. One more Grand-dad drink and I was through for the day. What a life!

Looking out of my sixth floor window I was amazed how they constructed their tall buildings here in town. There was a new building going up right across the street and they were using bamboo canes tied together for scaffolding. The workers were hurrying around, and going so fast that it made you want to look away, they were just too high.

I found some real good buys on gold rings and gold ear rings, some with Jade or Pearls. I would get lots of points with my wife with those.

Next to my last day here was when they had the bus tour set up to show the GIs what their island looked like. There was fifteen altogether, and some of those guys had their new girlfriends on their arms and the hotel let them come too, after all they were employees of the hotel. Everyone was in a laughing kind of mood, and Vietnam was far, far away.

Formosa proved to be very beautiful and the tour took us around some mountains and over on the eastern coast side. About three hours into the trip we stopped at a pretty beach where there was a restaurant, for our noon meal. They just happen to sell beer, and it made a good day better, after starting out perfect to begin with.

I could not help but notice the high mountain range west of this bit of paradise, and wondered if it was the one my crew nearly slammed into, or the one my friend hit a few years later?

Echoes of War

I really dreaded having to go once again to Danang AFB, but knowing it was just a short time and I would be heading home to the states then I was ready.

When I had gotten to the first six months of this tour, I put in for my base of choice, which was Little Rock AFB, Arkansas. To make sure that I would get it I also applied for retirement.

As soon as my plane arrived back in Vietnam, My R&R seemed like only a far away dream. Same old noise, same F4s (Fighter jets) taking off or landing every fifteen minutes, same sounds of big guns in the near distance, and as night fell, incoming rockets would shake the ground.

My assignment came in and it was for Little Rock AFB. It did not mention anything about retirement, so I went back to see the clerk that had wrote up my request. He remembered me and he said, "Yeah, I remember putting those papers right up here on this file cabinet, and by golly they are still here!"

I could hardly believe they sat there for nearly five months. I told him that I had gotten assigned where I wanted to go, so let's just tear up those papers for now.

My friend George had arrived on the same plane that I came in on, so we were to be leaving on the same one together scheduled for my birthday, the fifth of December. I just couldn't ask for a better birthday present than to be going home.

November the fifth came and so did our replacements that were to take our place. Both George and I worked for the same boss, and he called us in to tell us we were relieved from duty, that he would get in touch if he needed us.

Charles McCoy

Thirty days left and nothing to do, oh I still had my job at the theatre, but there was a big gap of time to just sit and think.

I picked up some colored felt pens and greeting card blank papers from the Base Exchange, and started my own greeting card company. These started out as just doodles for lack of something to do. They were just little cute drawings on the front page, and something funny when you opened it up.

I even had a name and card number on the back and near the bottom of each card. It read "Hallmark Hell No" Number 1 up to about 20, but the only thing wrong was as the number of the cards got higher, the dirtier they became. When I had the cards finished I just sat them up on the desk. George would pick them up, laugh then ask, "Can I send this to my wife? I said it was ok, but at that time I did not know that George and his wife and kids would drive into my drive way the second day after I got home.

After George introduced us, the first thing his wife said to me was, "You sure can draw!" I believe that was the first time in my life that I was at a loss of words. My wife told me that my face had never been that red, ever.

But that's getting ahead in time, and out of the war zone.

I started into reading western books and in just a few days I was into the third book, and really enjoying the Wild West in print.

One afternoon there was a lot of gunfire going on right outside our barracks. I walked into the laundry room and there sat George at a table in shorts and T shirt. He had ice in a bucket and it was cooling a bottle of Rum, also a bottle of coke. He was busy writing his wife and spoke to me but his train of thought was more on his letter.

The gunfire was coming at a faster pace and I looked out of the door to see what was going on. About one hundred yards away there was a guard tower this side of a tall chain link fence, and the guard had a firefight between

Echoes of War

him and whoever was in the tree line another couple hundred yards away. Our barracks just happened to be in line of fire from the shooter in the trees. A couple of rounds were getting too close and I kind of ran back towards George's table.

I told George, " My God there's a war out there!" and I no sooner got it out of my mouth than someone ran around the corner of our barracks and let go of an M-16 clip. I went under the table.

George acted like, "Well what are you doing under there man?"

"I repeated that there was a war going on out side!"

He casually got up and walked over to the door, at which time the light bulb over the door got blown into a thousand pieces.

He then said, "Move over!" as he joined me under the table.

It was along about this time of the year that a Marine Commander landed for an overnight visit. He was flying what looked like a brand new Marine Corp OV-10. They must have used ten pounds of wax just to shine that bird. It had to qualify, as the shiniest aircraft in the Air Force, beautiful was the word.

The plane was parked inside one of the concrete revetment that had the double steel wall running behind the back end of the structure. If any rocket were to come through that end, it would only have about an eighteen inch high by maybe four or five feet length to squeeze through that space.

The little church off base must have had its flag up for that night, you guessed it, and one rocket came through that little opening. That beautiful OV-10 was estimated to have received over seven hundred holes from that one rocket! It was a total loss.

155

Chapter Fifteen
Back to States and Retirement

The last few days of this year of battle were coming close to rotation back to the States. It just really wasn't as quick as we had in mind. The same worry was branded into our brains and had been there since the day that we arrived in this war zone. If you are going to die here, it will happen the first week, or your last week, so therefore and without your knowledge; you don't make any long range plans.

Packing proved to be no problem, and things like our small refrigerator, hot plate, and pots and pans, we just passed them on to our buddies that George and I had been sharing the dinner table with. With George's experience of cooking, I had put on about seven pounds of weight myself.

Finally my birthday arrived, which completed my year here, and it was the happiest of all my birthdays put together, because I was going home.

We had to get up and get to our departure point, and had to unpack and go through customs, before getting on the plane. Time seems to just be

Charles McCoy

dragging by, and so far this was turning out to be the longest day yet. But it was my birthday; by golly I was going to enjoy it.

Everybody aboard, and engines to max power, we were leaving the runway, and Danang AFB, Vietnam, and the war behind us. I came to a big decision in my life at this time, and in two words it was, "Prayer Works!"

After flying for awhile the pilot announced that we had just crossed the International Date Line, and we are now into yesterday. So I just had the shortest birthday yet, but that's all right I'll have another one come midnight! But wait, how old will I tell people that I am since I've had an extra birthday? Well I'm not going to worry about that, I'm just going to enjoy the ride.

We made a couple of refueling stops, and I had to change planes at Seattle, and most of the passengers on this plane were civilians. My ex-supervisor from Danang AFB was still heading the same way as me, so we both accepted a couple of Rum and Cokes from the Flight Stewardess to celebrate my extra birthday. I never drank much Rum, but I figured out that at altitude I believe that it must double its strength. I felt like I was flying just a little higher than this plane was.

Upon departing the aircraft at Little Rock, I was met by my wife and kids. After a few hugs and kisses, my smallest little girl said, "Guess what daddy, for my hits on the ball team, you owe me $26.75!" Everybody in the room probably was thinking that there is a happy family, from all the laughing we were doing. And they would have been right; also I still had twenty-five minutes left of my birthday.

When I left to go to Vietnam, The Air Force pay system lost my military pay record, and I received no pay for six months. Prior to coming home I wrote and told my wife that just in case, I was taking three month advanced

Echoes of War

pay so that would not happen again. Yep, you guessed it, no pay again for six months.

That's not all; it was three months before I saw the first ugly woman.

After a few days off I signed back into the base that I had left about fifteen months ago. It was funny when I was processing in at Wing Headquarters, I ran into my old supervisor from LRAFB who ask if I had been assigned to a squadron yet.

When I said no, he grabbed me by my arm and said, "Come on you are working for me!" At the same time he turned and opened the door to the Wing Commander's office, and we walked in where he announced to the Commander and his secretary, "This man is going to work for me!"

"Well ok Sergeant if you feel that way about it!" replied the Commander. At that moment my new-old boss came to attention and said "Sir!"

Everyone in the room roared with laughter.

A few more days of processing in and it was back to work for me. I had been in charge of running an OV-10 inspection phase dock for the first six months that I was in Nam so when my new-old boss learned that, he put me in charge of running his C-130 phase dock. I replaced a junior grade Technical Sergeant. He had positioned himself behind the status board desk, for his job duty of sitting at that desk, answering the phone and looking in charge.

My second day at work, I replaced him at his position with a man with three stripes, that could do that job; I had a supervisors position in mind for the Tech Sergeant. I gave him a clipboard and told him to follow me and I started showing him what to look for that the inspectors might find after our guys had completed their work. Any write up they found would be a black mark on us if we missed something.

Charles McCoy

After a week of carrying the clipboard, I found out the Tech Sergeant was unhappy with his job and volunteered to take over the responsibility of the "Alert Section".

A week later he told me that he just did not know what he got himself into. He had to personally sign for every piece of equipment on the flight line, and have it in painted areas, whenever the alert whistle blew so it could be loaded onto aircraft. It was a good twelve to fifteen hours a day job.

It all worked out, and we got to be real good friends after he found out that I really was trying to make his job easier.

I had not been in the States two months and all of a sudden they were talking of sending me to two months in Germany. I balked, and told them I had just put my paperwork in for retirement. They then got on another subject, and actually left me alone.

It was news to me too, for I had no idea of what I wanted to do to make a living in civilian life. Every time the thought came into my mind; I was sitting at my kitchen table looking at the sorry cabinets someone built on the job in my new house. I came to the conclusion that if whoever made these made a living doing that sort of work, I could learn to build a better set of cabinets and make even a better living.

In the process of doing all the paperwork of retirement, I found out I could be relieved four hours a day for three months from my AF duties, and go work in a cabinet shop to learn a new skill. That cabinet shop owner did not have to pay me anything since he was actually teaching me a trade. It worked out for both of us.

My first job turned out was to remodel my Squadron Commander's kitchen, where he lived off base. He seemed to be pleased with his new kitchen. He got a bargain, and he paid me a reasonable price, and gave me a lot of confidence in myself.

Echoes of War

Catch 22 hit like a tornado, when I discovered that I could build one set of cabinets in one week, by myself, but to load and install them, it took two people. So to make enough money to pay two salaries, you had to produce and install two sets in one week.

The Air Force gave me a "Physical" in the last week before I was to retire, and I should add the word "Fast" before the word Physical.

I went to the VA to check on getting a small business loan the first week after my discharge. I was told it had to go through a bank first then they would get behind it. Along come catch 22 again; you had to have collateral for the bank to take the chance. One thing though, the man from the VA ask, "Had I had a physical from the VA?"

I told him I had just got one from the Air Force.

He said "That one don't count, and if you ever had been on sick call, then I'm going to schedule you for a VA physical, so go along with me, you have nothing to lose."

Within the first thirty days, I reported in to the VA Hospital, where an X-ray revealed damage in my back. Then I had to go to a bone doctor who said I had infection in my lower lumbar, and it would turn into Degenerate Disk Disease, and would get worse as I aged, and it was from the C-130 door hitting me back in 1960. He and the VA rated me as Service Connected below 10 %, but when it got worse, then I should come back to get re-evaluated to a higher percentage. (No pay for Less than 10%)

To fast forward to April 25, 1980, I was going in and out of the VA with back problems and they were giving me pain medicine, and also the Disabled American Veterans also was behind me. In 1981, I became a Life Member of the DAV. They had also helped me put in a claim for a higher disability rating.

Charles McCoy

About then I felt as if I was falling apart, for I had not been able to do any lifting and had to hire help in my shop to build and install what we made. I just did the leg work of going out to measure and laying out the jobs on a board and paper. It took a total of five people, and they worked very well together.

Things got worse, the VA claim was turned down, and the base doctor I was seeing found a Thyroid Tumor, and it was confirmed at the VA hospital and that Little Rock AFB Hospital would do the operation. Then I had to check into the VA Hospital for a lung biopsy. They lost my X-rays and I was there for a week, but it turned out ok.

I was admitted to LRAFB Hospital May 12, 1982, for removable of nodule and RT Thyroid. Later on a VA claim for Agent Orange, all of this the VA claimed was denied and even went as far as saying I had never even complained with my Thyroid, nor that there was no evidence at the base for my operation.

I submitted a copy of the admittance slip to LRAFB Hospital, and I even have the scar on my throat for proof.

Time was flying by at a fast pace, and during a visit to El Reno, Oklahoma to see my Mother-in-law; I passed by the cities park where they had The Vietnam Memorial Moving Wall sit up. I made a copy of Walter's name onto paper, which I've copied below

As I stood before his name on that wall, I recalled that night when he came into my house in off-base Japan saying, "I know how we can make $5000!" We laughed about it then saying it wouldn't be worth going through a ditching to collect it. From a Pilot's goof up, that was actually a ditching of a C-130, only Walter did not make it. I wonder if the rest of the crew collected.

The Vietnam Veteran's Memorial Moving Wall

sept 18, 65

1959

OLE RYDER • BARRY N HAM
WALTER O TRAMEL •

OUR NATION HONORS THE COURAGE,
SACRIFICE, AND DEVOTION TO DUTY AND
COUNTRY OF ITS VIETNAM VETERANS.

1975

**El Reno, Oklahoma
June 1–8, 1997**

163

Charles McCoy

Each time that the VA turned me down, for disability I would go back to the DAV where they kept putting my Claim back into the appeals file. My back was getting worse, and they kept giving me pain medications. They had me to meet a board at one point, and it was one man and my DAV representative. The DAV again turned in my appeal for a higher disability percentage rating.

The Doctor at the VA Hospital gave me 400 pills of Ibuprofen each appointment I went to. I had to take two pills every four hours for pain in my back. They worked for two hours, and then I had to sit down for two hours before the next dose.

The reaction from them was loss of hair. There was an article in Good House Keeping magazine stating that Ibuprofen could cause loss of hair. To me it was like I was taking Chemo, so I tried cutting back on the dosage.

Next time at the VA doctor's visit she told me she could change to a stronger medicine but I would have to go to a wheel chair because I would be too drunk to walk. She also did not believe about the loss of hair, but it was the third item in the Medical Reaction book, but was written in Latin. She got mad because I was right and told me, "Well next time you get to hurting come back and I'll put you on the other meds."

I stopped going to the VA, and found a civilian Doctor and also a Chiropractor. Both gave me X-rays, and I had my back out of place in four spots. The Chiropractor adjusted my back, and it required going in twice a week for about a month and a half. I had relief and my new doctor started me on Arthrotec 50.

With this working, I was able to keep running my cabinet shop, but only in a supervisory position.

Echoes of War

The DAV kept running my paperwork, and we kept putting in for new appeals. It got to the point that I could barely close my briefcase, and it got too heavy for me to lift. Finally in 1996 my family Doctor told me, "Man you are disabled, you are not able to work, and you should put in for total disability."

I shut down my shop, and started selling off the shop tools and that kept me in groceries until I went on Social Security two years later. With a lawyer I was awarded full disability two years later, on Social Security.

The lawyer got me a physical with a Doctor from Social Security. His findings was that he agreed with the two VA Doctors that said I was totally and permanently disabled, but I was worse than they said I was.

By this time my claim file had reached VA in Washington. I received a letter telling me they were going to be handling my case. I was set up for a three part physical at the VA hospital, which I went through.

No word for a year, then I got the same letter I had received from the VA the year before, and I was to have a three part physical...again.

The Orthopedic Doctor who gave me that part of the exam, told me, "Man, your back is shot, but I'm, going to help you."

Then she must have gone home to write the report. She must have been watching JAG on TV, because she wrote that after the accident, "He got up off the deck and reported to the ship's dispensary."

I have never been on a ship in my life! And she even put in a statement that I was cured when I retired. This Doctor lied to me and on her report.

It gets worse when I received a letter from VA in Washington my claim would be turned over to an expert to determine my case.

I received a copy of the "EXPERTS OPINION" which had my file number and said that I was an 85 year old veteran who was shell shocked in 1943 in France."

Charles McCoy

I was only nine years old in 1943. I started once to put in a claim for not being able to remember that too!

I called VA in Washington and they wanted me to send that paperwork right back. I did, I made them a copy and sent that back. I believe this was a Hippa Violation.

February 2006, I went back in for two more VA exams. I had saw this one Doctor once before and he had gave me a report that I felt was in my favor. He again turned in a report that I felt would do the trick.

The other appointment was to see another Doctor that was to give me a "Tilt Test." When she saw how hard it was for me to get out of a chair and when walking down the hallway I nearly collapsed but caught myself against the wall she told me in her office, "I cannot give you that test, because you cannot stand for thirty minutes."

As I close my book down, I am awaiting the last word back from the Veterans Administration Management Section, Washington DC.

I have been told that this is the last time that I can appeal, and any father action I will have to pay my lawyers fee, and court cost. Then too, there is no more room in my briefcase for any more paperwork.

Any Serviceman reading this book, I strongly recommend that within the same month you are released from Service, you ask for and insist for a complete physical from the VA, and when you are turned down later in life, keep putting in appeal after appeal if nothing else, do it for Chuck.

When your appeal goes to Washington, and they Remand it back to the local VA for more exams and physicals where the catch comes into play, is when it gets back to Washington VA, your claim goes to the bottom of the list. When I called to check on mine, I was told they were three years behind, and sense mine was on the bottom, it would be another three years before it was looked at again.

Echoes of War

To put this into printed words, this writing started and was going down on paper over a two year period. My sweet wife had been diagnosed with lung cancer and through the ordeal of operations, hospitals, Chemo and rehab, there was some long spells of time between care-giving I started making notes for this book.

I had trouble trying to put into print how loud a rocket would sound. In truth it turned out to be loud enough that the Echoes of War last for thirty-five years, so far.

Finally a letter from the VA in Washington and they had made a decision. They were giving me Service Connection for Vasovagal Syncopal (Previously claimed as nervousness and blackouts) with 0 % assigned as of Mar29,1996. At the same time they had moved my "Less then 10%," they gave me in September 1972, up to 20%. Then on up to 40% as of January 11, 2003. They now call it, "Chronic Lumbar Sprain with Multilevel Degenerative Disc Disease."

Catch 22----As a serviceman, when you draw disability pay, for each dollar you get, they take a dollar back from your retirement pay. So therefore if you are 100% with disability, then you do not get your retirement pay, but the disability pay is higher.

One last exam from the VA, and that Doctor was to decide if I could go back to work. So far, there has not been an answer back from VA.

Dedication

In closing I would like to dedicate this book to my Wife, Wanda who I kept trying to get her to read this work as it progressed along. She said she would read it when I had finished writing it. That is what kept me going or else I would have put it down.

She passed away on May15[th] 2006, before this was finished, but I feel she had read this as we had lived it. My Friend, My Sweetheart, My Wife, My Love, My Life.

Wanda F. McCoy

Memorial to Walter Tramel

This is a picture of Walter Tramel and his wife Beverly as I remember them, they were a loving couple and very good friends to my family. Walter was an outstanding and remarkable man and would volunteer his services to anyone in need of a helping hand, even without their asking. It was knowing Walter that helped to give me the subject matter to even think of writing a book. He was a buddy and a friend, who is missed.

Printed in the United States
152363LV00003B/4/P